Intellectual Property in the Managerial Portfolio

Intellectual Property in the Managerial Portfolio

Its Creation, Development, and Protection

Thomas S. O'Connor

business**expert**
Press

Intellectual Property in the Managerial Portfolio: Its Creation, Development, and Protection

Copyright © Business Expert Press, 2012.

First published in 2012 by
Business Expert Press, LLC
222 East 46th Street, New York, NY 10017
www.businessexpertpress.com

ISBN-13: 978-1-60649-354-0 (paperback)

ISBN-13: 978-1-60649-355-7 (e-book)

DOI 10.4128/9781606493557

Business Expert Press Strategic Management collection

Collection ISSN: 2150-9611 (print)
Collection ISSN: 2150-9646 (electronic)

Cover design by Jonathan Pennell
Interior design by Exeter Premedia Services Private Ltd.,
Chennai, India

First edition: 2012

10 9 8 7 6 5 4 3 2 1

Printed in the United States of America.

Abstract

Intellectual property rights have been a part of the American pantheon of types of property rights since the very beginning of the nation, but using the term "intellectual property rights" to describe property rights is a new phenomenon dating back to the second half of the twentieth century. The need for intellectual property rights protection became extremely important and distinctly more difficult at that time as new technologies made it possible for unscrupulous "intellectual property pirates" to purloin, steal, or otherwise make off with the intellectual property of the unaware.

This book introduces the reader to the underlying logic of intellectual property rights, how one can acquire them, why they exist, the benefits derived from their ownership, and how they can be protected from unscrupulous persons. Legal and common sense alternatives that provide the keys to protection are outlined and instructions on their use are revealed.

The availability of intellectual property rights protection, both domestic and international, is outlined and discussed, as are the history of and the current trends relevant to the legal rights of the intellectual property owner and the limits of protection provided by the law and by extralegal alternatives of providing protection.

The author has published extensively in the field, and has been an expert witness in a number of significant legal cases in which the interpretation and application of intellectual property concepts were tested. He brings the benefit of this experience to the creation of this book.

Keywords

intellectual property, patents, copyrights, trademarks, trade secrets, contracts, dilution, infringement

Contents

Preface

The term "intellectual property" first appeared in European business literature in the middle of the nineteenth century referring to a certain type of asset. Its use gradually increased in frequency in that area as the century wore on, becoming better understood and crossing borders until international agreements defining the various sorts of intellectual property began to appear. By the 1880s, the concepts underlying the definition of intellectual property, the bases for the values of the various types of such property, and agreement in general on how such property might be protected to its owners became sufficiently well understood so that the Paris Convention of 1883 was confected to protect patent and related industrial property rights inclusive of trademarks, followed by the Berne Convention of 1886 targeted at the protection of copyrights.

The ensuing century showed much development in the breadth and coverage of the concepts covered by the international agreements related to intellectual property, despite the notable absence of the United States as a signatory of most of them and an equally notable conservatism on the part of the United States in extending coverage to property that in most international venues was recognized and protected as intellectual. This orientation began to change in the 1970s, and the United States has since become significantly involved in the international definition, development, and protection of intellectual property.

The following text examines, in a broad sense but with an essentially U.S.-based historical orientation, the concept of intellectual property as it is generally understood in the global sphere of business today.

Introduction

Intellectual Property, Its Definition, Its Worth, and Its Protection

Definition of Intellectual Property

A piece of intellectual property is most accurately described as an intangible creation that is the product of the human mind and to which can be assigned certain rights of property. Intellectual property may include, among many other things: (a) a unique new process to preserve foodstuffs for which a patent can be acquired, (b) a writer's book or article to which a copyright can be assigned, or (c) a distinctive label design (a trademark) that differentiates the products of its owner from those of other producers of similar goods. All of these examples and a number of other possibilities, by providing their owners with a monopoly, provide them with a significant advantage over competitors in the marketplace. The rights to intellectual property remain with the creator(s) of the property so long as they take appropriate action to prevent the usurpation of those rights by others.

The Value of Intellectual Property

The value of intellectual property to a company or individual is not based on the property's mechanical or physical properties because, for the most part, the form of property is a process, a document or alternative rendering of a concept, or a visual or graphic device. The value of intellectual property is based on the ownership of the property and the exclusive right to use, manufacture, reproduce, or create a unique object or concept based on that ownership. This exclusivity, which collaterally implies monopoly on the above-stipulated rights, gives the rights owner a uniquely protected position in the marketplace. As such, the ownership of intellectual property possesses the potential to be one of the most valuable assets a person or business can have.

Protecting Intellectual Property

Some would contend that the best way to protect intellectual property would be simply to keep it a secret, unrevealed to others. The difficulty with this point of view is that keeping secrets is quite possibly one of the most difficult human objectives to achieve. As a result of the recognition of this problem, over the past several centuries a body of law has developed to provide protection of their property to intellectual property owners. Intellectual property law is the area of the law that covers the protection afforded by patents, copyrights, trademarks, and trade secrets, as well as by employment contracts, and prohibitions of certain acts in other areas such as unfair competition.

In the United States, laws protecting intellectual property exist at both the state and federal levels. State laws cover a broad array of intellectual property fields ranging from trade secrets to the right of publicity. These laws differ from state to state.

At the federal level, laws confected based on the authority of the Constitution provide the basis for all national regulation involving patents and copyrights, and some of the legal bases for dealing with trademarks and unfair competition.

In addition to domestic laws designed to protect intellectual property rights, a number of international treaties provide additional protection. The Paris Convention for the Protection of Industrial Property (1883) was designed to protect patent rights, industrial designs, trademarks, and trade names in the international sphere. The Berne Convention for the Protection of Literary and Artistic Works (1886) was implemented to protect copyrights. These accords still provide the foundation for intellectual property rights protection internationally. Additional treaties, such as *The Madrid Treaty of* 1891 *and The Madrid Protocol of* 1989 as well as The Nice Agreement on the International Classification of Goods and Services for the Purposes of Registration of Marks have amplified the influence of these documents in recent years.

All of the above notwithstanding, the owner of a piece of intellectual property may still choose to protect it by keeping it secret either by literal secrecy (hiding it away) or by contracts with employees that may have to work with the secret property that commit them not to reveal the nature of the property.

PART I
Overview of Intellectual Property Concepts

CHAPTER 1

Intellectual Property Rights Protection

Legal Monopolies Granted by Government or Created by Private Action

Government-Granted Monopolies Described: Patents, Copyrights, and Trademarks

Though the three basic forms of government-protected intellectual property—patents, copyrights, and trademarks—differ in their concepts, purposes, and functions, they are alike in the fact that each confers upon its holder the unique right to use, transfer, and profit from the piece of intellectual property that is theirs.

Patents are government grants of monopoly that cover unique and useful discoveries in the sciences and breakthrough advances in the sphere of engineering. The source of the patented concepts is usually research based on physical principles. Patents are limited in duration, the term of utility patents in the United States typically being 20 years from the time application is filed for them. Patents must be applied for at and approved by the United States Patent and Trademark Office to become effective.

Copyrights arise out of the creative energy of writers, artists, and sculptors, as well as photographers, composers, musicians, and other performers who have produced unique tangible creations in their fields. Ownership of a copyright confers on the possessor the same rights of monopoly as does a patent to its owner. Copyrights are of significantly greater duration than are patents. A copyright, under the present U.S. law, runs from the date of the completion of the creation of the work to a date 70 years after the death of the last living "author" of the work. Though registration with the U.S. Copyright Office is no longer mandatory to secure copyright protection in the United States, it becomes necessary if one foresees the possibility of having to file an action for infringement of copyright in one of the federal courts of the United States, and thus may be the wiser course in any event.

Trademarks, which are in effect from the day on which they are first used for as long as the trademark remains in use, may endure for a very long time. There are a number of trademarks, domestically and internationally, that have been in existence for over 100 years. Trademark registration is not mandatory but registration does provide a broader scope of protection than does simple reliance on the common law protection otherwise provided by U.S. law.

The Nature of Patents

Growing out of a history over 500 years long, the granting of patent rights on scientific advances and unique applications of the mechanic arts (engineering technology) is an established policy of most governments. The first known patent granted in the English-speaking world was issued to John of Utynam in 1449, during the reign of King Henry VI of England, for a process of making stained glass.[1] The underlying concept of a patent as a monopoly authorized by government was institutionalized some 25 years later by the Patent Ordinance of Venice of 1474.[2] In Britain, the granting of patents became a legislative rather than a royal act in 1623 with the implementation of the Statute of Monopolies. Slightly over 150 years later, the U.S. Constitution accepted the theory of patent rights.[3]

The creators of inventions and discoverers of new scientific principles thus have the prerogative of asking their governments to award them for their accomplishments by giving them the exclusive right to exploit commercially what they have created or discovered. The logic behind the granting of "letters patent," as they were originally titled, or just plain patents, as they are now known, is to grant the innovators and discoverers of useful novelties the ability to recover the cost of the work that led to the innovation or discovery and to reap the often substantial financial benefits of the economic advancements that will result from their use while they are protected from competition—at least for some period of time.

United States Patent Law, a Brief History

In the United States, the Copyright Act of 1790 established a copyright term of up to 14 years, following in the path of the Statute of Monopolies by setting the upper limit rather than the specific duration of the grant. A new U.S. Patent Law, enacted in 1836, provided for a 7-year extension of the term of patent beyond the 14-year maximum under certain circumstances. Many minor revisions of the Patent Law were enacted between 1836 and 1870, when the next major change took place. The Patent Law of 1870 extended the term of patent to 17 years, where it remained until the late 1990s, when it was extended to 20 years.

Between 1870 and the turn of the twentieth century, an international treaty and several domestic laws of the United States had an effect on the concept of patents. The Paris Convention for the Protection of Industrial Property of 1883 articulated the general basis for patent protection among its signatories. It provided, for example, that if an individual applied for a patent in one's home country and that country was a member of the Convention, and followed the initial domestic application with the filing of an application in another country, also a member of the Convention, within a specified time, the effective date of filing in both countries would be the date of filing in the first country (the earlier date). The United States joined the Paris Convention on May 30, 1887.[4]

In 1887, the U.S. Interstate Commerce Commission Act was passed (24 Stat 379, Ch. 104.), followed in 1890 by the Sherman Antitrust Act (15 USC 1–7). The thrust of both these acts was to prohibit certain behaviors that tended to create monopolies in American business. The first law made it illegal for transportation companies (at that time predominantly railroads) to set rates that favored large-volume shippers over smaller-volume shippers while the second prohibited contracts, combinations, and conspiracies in restraint of trade as well as actual monopolies and attempts to monopolize any part of trade or commerce.

The philosophy of both these laws flew in the face of the idea of government-sponsored monopolies through patents, especially in the light of the use of patents by large companies in the last half of the nineteenth century to stifle competition. As a result, U.S. courts during the first half of the twentieth century tended to be rather unsympathetic to patent holders. During the second half of the century, the internationalization of American industry and the vast enlargement of the technology base led to changes in the relationship between the legislative and judiciary branches of government with respect to patents.

In 1994, as a result of the changes previously mentioned, the U.S. Patent Law was amended to comply with the Trade Related Aspects of Intellectual Property Rights (TRIPS) document, an agreement that had been attached to the Uruguay round of amendments to the General Agreement on Tariffs and Trade (GATT). The changes caused by the TRIPS also saw the extension, in 1995, of U.S. patent coverage for utility patents to 20 years, bringing them into conformity with the duration of patent coverage in most other countries. Reaction to the growth of the technology base also led to the broadening of the patentability of a number of plants, particularly sports, mutants, hybrids, and newly discovered seedlings by amendment of the Plant Patent Act of 1930. Computer programs that had at first been denied patent protection because they were interpreted to be mere mathematical algorithms, hence not "novel," were also allowed to seek patent coverage.

U.S. law at present provides for three types of patents: utility patents, those that follow the general definition of patent previously mentioned; design patents, limited to the aesthetic, visual, or architectural characteristics of a product; and plant patents, which cover newly created or discovered asexually reproduced plants. The normal duration of utility patents and plant patents is 20 years from the first date of filing, while duration of design patents is 14 years.

The Nature of Copyrights: Ownership of Creative Efforts by Their Creators—When Did It All Begin?

Publishing as an industry began when printed works became available in volume after the invention of the modern version of the printing press by Johannes Gutenberg in 1450. In those days, the rights to the works were usually deemed the property of the publisher, printer, or both rather than the author. For a time, northern Europe was the primary source of printed texts, with Britain lagging behind Continental progress. William Caxton, England's first publisher, was born to Philip and Dionisia Caxton in Kent sometime between 1414 and 1424.[5] After serving an apprenticeship to Robert Large, a wealthy mercer (dealer in luxury woven goods), in London between 1438 and Large's death in 1441, Caxton went into foreign trade, settling in Bruges in 1453. By then a successful merchant, he traveled to Burgundy where he became a part of the household of Margaret, Duchess of Burgundy, sister of the King of England. His travels ultimately found him in Cologne, where he observed the process of printing and was strongly influenced by the experience. He set up a press in Bruges, and there, in 1473, printed the first book to be published in English, *Recuyell of the Histories of Troye,* his own translation from the original French.[6] Three years later, Caxton established a press in Westminster in his homeland, and there he published an edition of *Canterbury Tales,* the first book to be actually printed in England. Caxton lived until at least 1491, serving as a printer and publisher until his death. At the time of his death, five other printers had established themselves in England.

As the number of printing presses in England grew during the late fifteenth century as a result of Caxton's pioneering work, the government sought to control the publishing industry by granting a monopoly on book printing and sales to printers. There the matter remained until after the English Revolution of the mid-seventeenth century. The Licensing Act of 1662 solidified the monopoly on publishing, placing its administration in the hands of the Stationers' Company, a guild of printers authorized to censor publications and to publish those they considered acceptable.[7]

Copyrights Pass From Printers Into the Hands of Authors: British and U.S. Copyright Laws

Reservation to an author rather than a publisher of the right to income derived from his or her work, a concept similar to that of the patent, harks back to the reign of Queen Anne of England. When the English Licensing Act of 1662 expired in 1695, it was not renewed. In 1710, the

Statute of Anne[8] was enacted. This law, named after its sponsor Queen Anne, vested the title and right to copy and publish written works with their authors rather than with publishers. It also set the term of copyright at 14 years, renewable, if the author still lived at the end of the first term, for an additional 14 years.

The U.S. Constitution placed copyrights in the same essential category as it did patents. They were and are authorized by Article I, Section 8, Clause 8 of the document, in which the Congress is endowed with "the ... power ... to promote the progress of science and useful arts, by securing for limited times to authors and inventors the exclusive right to their respective writings and discoveries."

The U.S. Copyright Act of 1790 was modeled on the Statute of Anne. It offered the same terms of copyright as did that statute. The 1831 revision of the 1790 law extended the term of copyright from 14 to 28 years, renewable for another 14 years. The extension applied both to works not yet published and to those whose copyrights had not expired.

Little of note happened in the United States with regard to copyright for the next 68 years except that, in 1870, administration of the Copyright Act moved from the individual federal district courts to the Library of Congress Copyright Office. On the world stage, however, a number of significant events occurred. In 1886, the Berne Convention was enacted. This treaty became the basis for mutual recognition of copyright between nations. It has been revised five times since 1886. In 1908, the Berlin Revision set the duration of copyright at the life of the (last living) author of a work plus 50 years. In the United States, not yet a member of the Berne Convention, the duration of copyrights became 28 years renewable for another 28. The U.S. Copyright Act was revised in 1976 to reflect significant changes in the technology of printing, the desire to protect performance rights, and new communication media in anticipation of the United States ratifying the Berne Convention. The terms of copyright were made the same as those called for by the Berlin Revision except that works for hire were protected for a maximum of 75 years. The kinds of things covered by copyright were expanded to include recordings of musical and other works (performances), certain types of graphic creations, and new kinds of media. The United States became a signer of the Berne Convention in 1988, 102 years after its initial implementation.

In 1998, Congress passed the Sonny Bono Copyright Term Extension act. This act extended the term of copyright from the life of the last living author plus 50 years to the life of the last living author of a work plus 70 years. Holding the copyright to a work that has achieved popularity, especially now in the era of vast accessibility of entertainment devices that not only play music on the fly but also allow one to read books and show movies on handheld devices, amplifies the profitability of any copyrighted work, whether written or performed.

The Nature of Trademarks: Beginning at the Beginning

Trademarks are quite likely the oldest form of intellectual property. It is apparent that animal marking, in the form of heat branding or some other way of distinguishing the animals of one herdsman from another, was practiced as early as 5,000 years before the current era (BCE). Indeed, the cave paintings at Lascaux in the Dordogne, France, show bison with symbols on their flanks presumed to be ownership marks.[9]

The evidence of the existence of trademarks is present in Mesopotamia in 3500 BCE in the form of cylindrical seals used as signatures on the fired clay documents of that period. Five hundred years later, bricks, pottery, quarry stones, and roof tiles from Egypt bore ownership and makers' marks. The author has personally observed water pipes in Greece that have been reliably dated to 2500 BCE and bear plainly visible makers' marks. This practice of marking fired-clay goods has continued from that time to the present. Some brickmakers still stamp their products with their names or other identifying marks before firing.

Trade Dress as a Form of Trademark

Today, a special class of trademarks, known as trade dress, continues in the tradition of these very early marks. Consisting of concepts such as the shape of the container in which a product is packaged or the container's color or even the color of the product itself, pictorial representations identifying absent words that might ordinarily be attached to a product or service, architectural or design features, both exterior and interior, which create the "ambiance" of a business, and even unique sounds, such as musical themes and the recorded roar of a lion, are claimed as trade dress and treated as trademarks. Trade dress has the potential to act as a strong differentiator of a company's products and services, and even of the firm itself, thus enhancing profitability. Trade dress will be discussed at length in Chapter 7 in the context of its increasing use in recent years.

Evolution of the Common Trademark

By the tenth century of the current era (CE or AD), "merchants' marks" or "proprietary marks" appeared. Applied both to goods and their packaging, their essential purpose was to prove ownership of goods that had been lost in shipwrecks and subsequently recovered by salvage operators. In Britain, swords were marked with what would now be called "proof marks" so that if they failed in service their makers could be brought to account for any untoward injury their user might have sustained.[10] The marks also served as quality indicators for those blades and other "proved" items of military hardware so that reliable makers of durable products could be favored with further orders for similar products. Markings on the crates in which such goods were shipped also served to identify products and their makers. The English enacted basic trademark laws in the thirteenth century to prevent the copying of the products of one company by another, thus protecting reliable manufacturers. With the growth of the guild system in Europe in the fourteenth and fifteenth centuries, "hallmarks" appeared attesting to the source and quality of certain products such as silver and gold ware, porcelain, and other expensive and saleable property. The Industrial Revolution of the late eighteenth century caused the guild system to collapse and "free enterprise" supposedly reigned. However, existing British statutes against forgery, counterfeiting, and fraud were brought to bear against infringers of trademarks, converting the effect from criminal prosecution to civil litigation by the common law process of precedential evolution.[11] The English "broad arrow," first used to mark small arms and artillery as British crown property in the mid-sixteenth century, is still used to mark the modern versions of those items today.

Trademark acknowledgment and protection was late coming in the United States, the first Federal Trademark Act being published in 1870. The 1870 Act was amended in 1878 but was soon struck down by the Supreme Court (100 U.S. 82) (see also)[12] on the basis that, in passing the 1878 law, the Congress exceeded the powers granted it by the Patent and Copyrights Clause of the Constitution (Art. 1, Sec. 8, Cl. 8). A new law was enacted in 1881 based for its authority on the Interstate Commerce Clause (Art. 1, Sec. 8, Cl. 3) of the Constitution. This, too, was abolished in short order, to be replaced in the same year by yet another law based on the same clause. This law, though more successful than the previous two, could not keep up with the rate of growth of the American economy and was therefore subjected to major amendment in 1905 and subsequent amendments periodically until it was replaced by the Lanham Act (15 USC 1052 et seq.) in 1946.

The Lanham Act and American Trademarks

The Lanham Act has been extensively amended since its passage, but remains the definitive federal source of trademark protection in the United States. It is not, however, the only source of protection for trademarks in the United States. Since the Lanham Act covers only products that are sold in interstate commerce, vendors whose goods, services, or both are marketed solely within a single state may seek protection under the trademark law of that state. One provision that does NOT exist in the Lanham Act is mandatory registration of a trademark if its owner wishes to receive basic protection if the item is traded in interstate commerce. A trademark receives protection under common law (clarifies the statement) if its proprietor can demonstrate that he or she or his or her legal predecessor was the first person to use the mark and it has been used continuously since that date. There are a number of other conditions that apply to receiving trademark protection that will be covered in Chapter 6, among which are the roles of the principal and supplemental registers in the enrollment of registered trademarks, how one asserts claim to a trademark or service mark, and supplementary laws related to trademarks such as the Trademark Dilution Act of 1995 and the Trademark Dilution Revision Act of 2006.

Nongovernmental (Private) Creation of Legal Monopolies: Trade Secrets

It is not mandatory that an individual or firm seek a patent on a scientific discovery or an engineering advance they have discovered or created, nor is it necessary that a person seek a copyright on an original document or other work of literature or art he or she may have created. The law provides them the opportunity, but they cannot be forced to avail themselves of it.

One might believe that failure to seek protection from the law for such intellectual property would be a foolish act, but let us examine the matter further. To apply for a patent, it is necessary that the applicant provide the patent office with a complete description of the scientific discovery or invention, what it does, how it does it, how it can be made, what kind of equipment is needed, and so forth. You might think that, if you were in such a position, you would not want potential competitors to know how you make the subject of your discovery. Even should you secure a patent on the process, you should keep in mind at least one old saw relevant to the issue of patents: "what one good engineer can design, another can redesign in 2 or 3 years." This states the risk that a patent may become relatively worthless in a short time.

Some scientists and engineers, therefore, choose to keep their discoveries and designs secret. Of course, something isn't secret even if only one person knows what it is. Therefore, the next best thing is to have only one person who knows the nature of the discovery or the design (assuming discovery means scientific finding and design implies engineering advancement). Historically, the kinds of things that have been successfully held as trade secrets have been formulas that have been possible to divide into parts and the parts held secret separately. Trusted persons knew parts of the formulas and, when batches of product were needed, would share their knowledge to mix appropriate quantities of the components of which they were knowledgeable.

The formula for Coca-Cola concentrate is perhaps the most famous trade secret in the world. Some allege that no one knows the complete formula and that very few employees of the company have access to the process by which it is confected. Those who believe this story hold that any attempt to analyze the ingredients of the completed mix, for instance by heating, will cause decomposition of it into its elemental parts, making remixture impossible. No one knows for sure the truth of these allegations. It began to be rumored in early December 2011, however, that the secret formula for the beverage concentrate had been moved from the vault in SunTrust Bank of Atlanta where it had been kept since 1925 to a special facility in the World of Coca-Cola exhibition in the same city. This was confirmed by a press release from Coca-Cola Company on December 8, 2011, the opening date of the Vault of the Secret Formula.[13] The move was covered worldwide in print and broadcast media.

It is also widely believed that the basic recipe for Cracker Jack candy is known only in parts to trusted employees of the company. In this case, the five ingredients—molasses, popping corn, peanuts, salt, and a small amount of vegetable oil—are believed to be placed into an autoclave-like device and mixed together under a certain mixture of pressure, temperature, and rotation, controlled by an automatic process, until the well-known candy is produced. Based on a popular but sticky confection invented by the Chicago candy firm of F. W. Rückheim and Brother and sold at the 1893 Chicago World's Fair, the product ultimately to be known as Cracker Jack suffered some early problems due to its stickiness. The process that got rid of the stickiness was secretly developed in 1896 by Louis Rückheim, brother and business partner of Frederick William Rückheim, the company's founder, and remains a treasured trade secret today.[14]

Both the Coca-Cola and Cracker Jack formulas have remained secret for over a hundred years and both have generated very substantial revenues for their proprietors, thus demonstrating that, under carefully maintained circumstances, keeping a product formula secret may well be the best course. Any patent that these two formulas may have received would have long since expired.

Obviously, there is a substantial risk in attempting to keep a trade secret truly secret. One method of protecting those things that a firm wishes to keep secret is to assure that all those persons who might have need to know all or parts of those secrets sign rigorous nondisclosure agreements thereby preventing them, subject to substantial penalties similar to those mentioned in the next paragraph, from revealing any part of that knowledge to anyone else.

Employment Contracts: The Employee Sworn to Secrecy

Some firms have been known to write employment contracts with employees who are to be trusted with the development of products the composition or physics of which are desired to be kept secret, which include "secrecy clauses," forms of nondisclosure agreements, under which the revelation by the employee of any information specified as the employer's exclusive property results in draconian penalties being enforced against the employee. The employer usually includes in such agreements financial and, possibly, other penalties that the employee is informed of at the beginning of his or her employment, which strongly argue against his or her revealing the secret information. It is, of course, the obligation of the employer to enforce the special conditions and penalties included in employment contracts.

Summary

Intellectual property rights as defined in this chapter are protected by three forms of government-granted monopolies—patents, copyrights, and trademarks. Alternatively, they may be protected by legal monopolies created by private action in the form of trade secrets and employee contracts that bind employees to secrecy with respect to certain aspects of their work. Patents have a history in English-speaking countries dating back to the middle of the fifteenth century. The exclusive right to produce printed materials, the copyright, followed the invention of the printing press, at first giving the right of publication to the printers, rather than the authors, of books and other printed materials. It was not until the early eighteenth century that the copyright passed from the printers to the authors of printed works. The U.S. Copyright Act of 1790 was modeled on the British Statute of Anne. Trademarks have a history dating back to significantly before the modern era of history. They were originally and still are designed to protect the relationship between vendors of specific products and their products. Trade secrets, as the name implies, usually refer to recipes, formulas, or processes used in the making of a product that the proprietor wishes to keep from becoming known by outsiders. They are often used in lieu of a patent because, in order to acquire a patent, one must reveal to the government the very things that a trade secret usually seeks to protect. Employee contracts that swear the employee to secrecy with respect to certain aspects of their work go hand in hand with trade secrets, in that they provide a vehicle by which the trade secret is acknowledged to be a trade secret but protected by a binding legal promise not to be revealed.

CHAPTER 2

The Mechanics of Acquiring Intellectual Property Protection From Government Sources

The Process of Acquiring a Patent

The process of acquiring a patent is the lengthiest, most expensive, and the most detailed of all the protocols involved in securing government-provided protection for intellectual property rights. Success in obtaining a patent, however, often means that one has acquired a very valuable asset in the form of a monopoly on a unique scientific achievement or an engineering breakthrough. Weighing the cost of acquiring the patent versus the revenue likely to be earned from it often strongly argues for the expenditure of the funds to secure patent protection.

The following steps are necessary if a patent is to be sought. Though there is no legal requirement that a patent applicant retain legal counsel, the necessary sequence of activities involved in securing a patent (listed in the following text) strongly argues for retention of a good patent attorney.

1. Verify the novelty of the discovery or engineering advance
   The basic necessity in laying the foundation for the acquisition of a patent is to develop an advancement in the engineering arts or a discovery in science that is "novel" (unique—never before seen), "replicable" (can be done over and over again consistently), and has "utility" (potential value in industry or commerce). In general, the more revolutionary the development or discovery, the more valuable it

will be in commerce and hence the more valuable will be the possession of a patent to its creator or discoverer. The would-be proprietor
of the subject of the patent must therefore make every effort to insure
that the subject of the application is novel and of significant merit.

It is not sufficient that the advance or discovery that is likely to
be patented be theoretically possible. It must be demonstrable that
it does, in fact, do what it is alleged to be capable of doing. In this
connection, it may be necessary to construct a working model of the
subject of the possible patent.

2. Conduct a patent search to determine whether there is prior application or patent
Once it has been determined that the advance or discovery that is
to be patented meets the requirements of novelty, replicability, and
utility, the would-be-grantee must conduct a patent search to make
sure that the claimed innovation has not been patented previously.
Any prior patent, whether current or expired, that claims the same
coverage as the subject of the current application for patent takes
precedence and will make the current application null and void. If
this is the case, it becomes necessary either to give up on the idea of
patenting the supposed innovation or to explore the possibility of
devising a new innovation different from the first.

If the patent search shows no conflicting patents or current applications, the application for a patent may then be created. In connection with this, it is important to recognize that, if the existence of the
basis for the patent application is revealed to anyone, especially in a
commercial context, then one has only a year to complete and file
the application with the patent office unless each and every person
and organization to which the existence of the discovery has been
mentioned signs a nondisclosure agreement.

3. Develop the patent application
A patent application consists of four parts:
A. The specification, which explains the discovery or advancement
so that an individual knowledgeable in the field of the invention
could make and use it without any further experimenting;

B. The claims, which state exactly what advancements or discoveries the application seeks to protect. Because they lay out the exact scope of the coverage claimed, the claims are the most crucial part of the application;

C. The abstract, which verbally summarizes the specifics of the workings of the claimed discovery or advancement, its functional components and their interrelationships;

D. The drawings, which, in addition to the abstract, provide all the necessary information to facilitate physical duplication of the original working model. Drawings may not be necessary in the case of purely chemical or microphysical phenomena.

4. Submit the patent application

On receipt of the application, the Patent Office will assign it an application number and will return to the applicant a notice of date of receipt. A Patent Examiner will be assigned to the application, and he or she will communicate with the applicant concerning each issue or question that arises in the examination of the patent application. The interactive communication between the applicant and the Patent Examiner will ultimately determine the nature and scope of the finalized patent, if one is granted. This process often takes as much as 3 years. The Patent Office has rigorous standards of form and presentation for both text materials and drawings. The applicant should familiarize himself or herself with these standards before submitting the application for a patent.

The Cost of Obtaining a Patent: Three Examples

Acquiring a patent can be a quite an expensive endeavor. While, on their face, the activities involved in the process explained above do not explicitly call for any legal training, it is nonetheless true that the majority of people who file applications for patents, recognizing the detailed, technical, and complex nature of the process, avail themselves of the services of patent attorneys to assist in their efforts.

In a recent online article,[1] Gene Quinn, founder of IPWatchdog, Inc., and an attorney with the firm of Zies, Widerman and Malek, has estimated the total cost of acquiring patents on three devices, assuming the use of legal counsel in the preparation:

1. First Device: A computer-implemented method for facilitating certain functionality via the Internet
   A. Patent search with detailed patentability assessment $2,400
   B. Preparation of nonprovisional patent application $14,000
   C. Filing fee for nonprovisional patent application $1,200
   D. Professional illustrations to accompany application $400
   Total Cost $18,000

2. Second Device: Consumer electronics product
   A. Patent search with detailed patentability assessment $2,000
   B. Preparation of nonprovisional patent application $9,500
   C. Filing fee for nonprovisional patent application $800
   D. Professional illustrations to accompany application $400
   Total Cost $12,700

3. Third Device: Mechanical tool
   A. Patent search with detailed patentability assessment $1,600
   B. Preparation of nonprovisional patent application $8,000
   C. Filing fee for nonprovisional patent application $600
   D. Professional illustrations to accompany application $400
   Total Cost $10,600

All other things being equal, if a patent is granted, its coverage runs from the date on which its application was filed. There are, however, certain exceptions to this rule. If the Patent Office takes an extraordinarily long time to process the patent application before granting the patent, additional duration of coverage may be granted to compensate for the delay. In very rare instances, conflicts arising out of the coverages of two or more patents may involve contests that may ultimately result in cross-licenses of the conflicting elements of the patents, which effectively extend the patents' durations.

In the late 1950s, the first integrated circuit was developed by two independent researchers simultaneously, Jack Kilby at Texas Instruments and Robert Noyce at Fairchild Semiconductor. Both of them received patents for their very similar efforts, resulting in several years of legal battles that ended in a successful cross-license compromise. Despite this conflict, both men's careers remained very successful, Royce going on to cofound Intel, and Kilby ultimately receiving the U.S. National Medal of Science in 1970 and the Nobel Prize in Science in 2000.

Once a patent is granted, the patent holder must pay maintenance fees that fall due in the 4th, 8th, and 12th years of the patent's duration. These fees increase with the passage of time and are also higher if the patent holder is a large entity (big organization) rather than a small entity. Items manufactured under the patent also typically cite their patent coverage by a statement such as the following (U.S. Patent 4,550,523) cast or etched for permanence into the product material as a notice of the existence of a patent claim. On occasion, several patents may be listed.

The Process of Acquiring a Copyright: It's Certainly Simpler Than Getting a Patent

1. What things are subject to copyright?

    Copyrights are designed to protect the exclusive rights to publication of "original works of authorship" that are "fixed in a tangible form of expression." The U.S. Copyright Law is Title 17 of the United States Code. It defines "tangible form" as any physical method of retention, which can be perceived directly or with the use of a machine or device. A motion picture stored on a Digital Video Disk (DVD) qualifies as being in tangible form because it can be perceived when played on an appropriate piece of equipment.

    Works capable of being copyrighted include the following original efforts:

    A. literary works;

    B. musical compositions, including accompanying words;

    C. dramatic works, including accompanying music;

    D. pantomimes and choreographic works;

    E. pictorial, graphic, and sculptural works;

    F. motion pictures and other audiovisual works;

    G. sound recordings; and

    H. architectural renderings.

The listed categories are typically interpreted broadly for purposes of copyright. Thus, computer programs and most "compilations" may be registered as "literary works," while maps and architectural plans may be registered as "pictorial, graphic, and sculptural works."

Works that cannot be copyrighted are facts, ideas, systems, or methods of operation (such as how a machine works), but copyrights may be used to protect descriptions of these things.

2. Should claims to copyright be registered?

The protection of copyright begins immediately from the moment of creation of the work and its reduction to a tangible form. If it can be proven that the work was finished on a specific date at a specific time, the author's rights to that work are protected from that instant. If the work is NOT registered, the burden of proof of these requirements lies with the claimant of the protection. Though registration of a copyright is not mandatory, it confers a number of specific benefits upon the copyright holder:

A. It establishes a public record of the copyright claim.

B. It is a precondition for filing an infringement claim in federal court for works of U.S. origin.

C. If the registration is completed before or within 5 years of the publication of the work, it provides prima facie (on its face) evidence of the validity of the copyright claim and of the validity of the facts stated in the copyright certificate in the court.

D. If registration occurs within 3 months after the publication of the work or prior to an infringement of the work, statutory damages and attorney's fees can be claimed by the copyright owner in court actions.

E. Registration of the copyright allows the copyright owner to record the registration with the U.S. Customs Service for protection against importation of infringing copies of the work.

3. When and how can copyright registration be accomplished?

In the United States, the Library of Congress is the agent for copyright registrations. At the time of this writing, the duration of a copyright is the life of the last living author of a work plus 70 years.

No one but the author of the work or a licensee of the author of the work can profit from or copy the work during the duration of the copyright. The term author refers to all the participants in the creation of the work. No single author from a team of authors may grant a license to a nonauthor; all living participants in the authorship must approve the action (see www.us.copyright.gov for complete, up-to-date details).

Registration of a copyright for a work need not be made immediately on the completion of the work. It may be done any time within the term of the copyright. In the United States, copyright registration may be accomplished in two ways: by the traditional paper document method or by using the Copyright Office eCO online system.

To register a work in the United States using paper documents, three things must be sent in the same envelope or package to:

Library of Congress Copyright Office
101 Independence Avenue
Washington, D.C. 20559-6000.

1. One of the following forms, as appropriate:
   A. for literary works and computer programs—Form TX
   B. for performing arts—Form PA
   C. for single-issue series/periodicals—Form SE
   D. for a group of issues of serials/periodicals—Form SE/Group
   E. for a group of daily newspapers or newsletters—Form SE
   F. for sound recordings—Form SR
   G. for visual arts—Form VA

2. A nonreturnable filing fee for each application. At present (mid-2012) the basic fee is $35, but may vary depending on how filing is undertaken. It is a good idea to check the amount for each case.

3. A nonreturnable copy (the deposit copy) of the work being registered. The deposit requirements will differ from case to case. The deposit is usually one copy of an unpublished work or two copies of a published work for which registration is sought.

Failure to submit all the required copies, audio recordings, or identifying material will result in the Copyright Office NOT processing the application for registration and the submitted materials will not be returned. If a published work has appeared in more than one edition, send the best version as your deposit copy. If the deposit requirements in a case are in doubt, the applicant should check with each category of work involved in *Copyright Registration Procedures*, the Copyright Office's official guidebook.

To file an application using the eCO System, the applicant should log on to http://copyright.gov/eco/. The website can help determine the correct procedures, proper forms, and current fees and other requirements. Application for a copyright registration is by far the simplest of the processes for securing legal protection for intellectual property.

4. What happens next?

If all of these requirements are fulfilled, the applicant will ultimately receive in the mail a certificate of registration of the copyright. It is not necessary for the registered (often said to be copyrighted) work to be published, but for most authors this is the primary objective. A notice of copyright is ordinarily appended to the copyrighted work, the most common method being to list the copyright symbol ©, the date of the copyright, and the copyright owner's name in some visible location near the beginning of the work (such as in the following: "Copyright© 2010 by Brace and Bit Publishing Company, Inc.").

Acquiring Trademarks: Choosing From Among Three Processes

1. Trademarks and Common Law

In some countries, registry of trademarks is mandatory in order for the trademark holder to claim the protection available to the mark under the law. Most countries whose legal system is based on code or civil law have such a requirement. The United States, being a common law country, provides protection for trademarks without registration.

The simplest way to acquire rights to a trademark in the United States is through the operation of common law. The definition of a trademark is very straightforward. A trademark is a word, symbol, or phrase used to identify a particular manufacturer or seller's products and distinguish them from the products of another (15 USC 1127). It should be recalled that, ultimately, trademark law protects MARKS. Such marks may be written words or phrases, symbols such as a picture of the product for which the trademark is claimed, or a device such as a graphic figure with some relationship to product function—or of no real representational value, so long as they differentiate one firm or person's goods from those of another.

2. Registering trademarks in the United States—statutory registration state by state

Though it is not mandatory, trademarks may be registered in each of the states of the United States and in the District of Columbia. Registering a trademark in a single state or in the district secures protection for it in that state or the district alone. In most states, trademark registry is a function of the Department of State. A few states and the District of Columbia have separate departments for the purpose. To determine the specific requirements for registering a trademark in a specific state, this site is the place to start the FindLaw Website.[2] While the basic requirements in each state's case are similar to those outlined for the common law unregistered trademark, there may be specific details to be considered for each state or the federal district.

3. National Trademark Registration with the Patent and Trademark Office of the U.S. Department of Commerce

If a trademark is likely to be used in interstate commerce or in foreign trade, it usually serves the best interests of the owner to register it on a national basis. Registration of a trademark in the United States requires making an application to the U.S. Patent and Trademark Office (PTO). In general, the contextual requirements for registering a trademark with the federal Trademark Office are similar to those of acquiring basic protection by common law. The process itself is somewhat like that of applying for a patent. The trademark office, in fact, recommends that the applicant seek legal counsel so as to avoid making errors in the process. On their informational website (www.uspto.gov/trademarks/index.jsp) they make it a point to note that the USPTO only registers trademarks, they do not police them.

A. The first step in registering a trademark is to decide how your mark is to be depicted. A clear representation of the mark must be filed with the application. There are two ways to represent one's mark: (a) standard character format or (b) stylized or design format. The standard character format is used when it is desired to register words, letters, numbers, or any combination thereof, without claim to any particular font style, size, color, and absence of any design (graphic) element. The standard format provides broad rights, including use in any manner of presentation. The stylized format, alternatively, is appropriate when the intent is to register a mark with a design element, words, or letters having a particular stylized appearance. Both formats cannot be mixed in one mark. If each is desired to be used, this constitutes two marks and the two must be presented and applied for separately. Once acquired, marks of either or both forms can be used on the same product.

B. The second step in securing trademark registration is to identify clearly the precise goods and services to which the mark will be applied. The identification must be specific enough to identify the nature of the goods and services for which the mark(s) are desired. This website domiciles the *Acceptable Identification of Goods and Services* Manual of the Trademark Office.[3]

The *International Schedule of Classes of Goods and Services*[4] at (www.uspto.gov/trademarks/trademarks/notices/international.jsp) may also be helpful in identifying goods and services for trademark registration purposes. It identifies all of the headings of the international classes of trademarks and provides explanatory notes concerning what each class does and does not include. The class headings by themselves, however, are not acceptable for registration purposes.

C. The next (third) step toward registering a trademark is a search of the PTO database of existing and pending marks at the Trademark Office's TESS (Trademark Electronic Search System) site located at the USPTO site.[5] Such a search can be conducted free of charge and will reveal whether anyone is already claiming trademark rights to a particular mark. If the mark that is desired to be registered contains a design element, it will be necessary to search for its design code at the USPTO site.[6] This is the site of the *Design Code Search Manual.* If the TESS search yields a mark that appears to be in conflict with the desired mark, only marks classed as "live" are in a position to block an application for registration. "Dead" marks cannot do so.

The above searches will not discover trademarks that have not been registered with the PTO. Additional searches may be necessary, such as those of the trademark database of the state of domicile of the firm seeking to register the trademark, *Thomas Register of Goods and Services,*[7] and the *Dot.com Directory of Businesses.*[8] It might also be wise to simply access several search engines and enter the desired trademark's written component.

It is important to exercise due diligence at this point so as to avoid a later suit or suits for trademark infringement or unfair competition. In this connection, the findings of all the searches undertaken should certainly be retained, and an affidavit from legal counsel attesting to the extent of the search(es) conducted might be helpful.

D. The Proper Basis of the Trademark Application

On completion of the trademark search, the next (fourth) step toward registration is the selection of the proper basis for application. The most likely choices are the "use in commerce" or the "intend to use in commerce" basis. In either case, the applicant must demonstrate prior to registration that he or she has used the mark in commerce. Commerce in this context is classified as interstate, territorial, or between the United States and a foreign country.

If the mark for which registration is being applied has already been used in commerce, the application may be filed under the "use in commerce" basis. If the mark has not yet been used, but its use is planned, the "intend to use in commerce" basis is appropriate. Evidence of such intent must be substantive, that is, it must be clear that the mark will be used in the foreseeable future—a clear example of which would be that a firm is in the start-up phase with assets, a business plan, and other activities appropriate to preparing to use the mark. If an "intend to use" application is filed, then an additional form and filing fee must be paid prior to registration that are not required if the "use in commerce" basis is elected. Evidence of use in commerce is demonstrated by definitively establishing the date of first use of the mark anywhere as well as the date of first use in commerce. An example of the use must also be provided. The Berne Convention, the ruling international treaty concerning trademarks, provides that under certain conditions one may file application for trademark registration in the United States based on a foreign application, foreign registration, or international registration.[9]

E.   Filing the application for registration of a trademark

Actually, filing the application for registration, the fifth step in the trademark application process, is most efficiently handled using the *Trademark Electronic Application System*.[10] The form can be filled out and filed entirely online. It is also possible to preview the application form at the USPTO Website[11] so that the applicant can determine exactly what information will be required on the final form.

It is still possible to file for registration of a trademark using a paper form. This form can be obtained from the Trademark Assistance Center at toll-free number 1-800-786-9199. It is better to note ahead of time that processing of a paper form is slower than processing an electronic application.

F. Fees involved in filing an application for trademark registration
    The above-mentioned fees are based on three factors:
    (i)   the number of marks being requested. A separate applica-
          tion must be filed for each mark;
    (ii) the number of classes per application. More than one class
          of good may appear on a single application;
    (iii) the form being used to file the application. Submission
          using the TEAS Plus form costs $275 per class of goods
          or services listed but the filing requirements are rigid;
          submission using the regular TEAS form costs $325 per
          class but is more flexible. Detailed information about fees
          can be found at the following site: http://www.uspto.gov/
          trademarks/tm_fee_info.jsp[12]

Filing fees are nonrefundable, even if no registration is forth-
coming.

Basics of Trademark Use

If one places a trademark in use, the convention is to identify the product
to which it is applied as being trademarked in one of two ways. If the trademark is NOT registered, the following type of notice is usually used (Southern Maid™ Smoked Sausage) where the words "Southern Maid" are being
claimed. If the mark were registered, the following style would be typical
(Snow Queen® Ice Cream). This latter is a small upper-case R in a circle
identifying the words "Snow Queen" as the mark. If graphics were involved,
the same marks would be used in connection with them. Service marks
work the same way except for the use of the letters "sm" instead of "tm."

1. What determines how a trademark looks?
   A vast array of possibilities arise that might serve as a firm's trademark. In the United States, tangible products and intangible products may be trademarked; however, the intangible products bear
   what are known as "service marks" to differentiate them from the
   marks applied to tangible goods. In general, trademarks and service marks must be "unique," that is, substantially different from

any other trade or service mark used in the venue in which the subject mark is to be found. Henceforth, the term trademark will be used to apply to either trade or service marks unless otherwise noted.

2. Peripheral trademark types supplement the basic forms.
   A. Trade names are marks used to identify a business rather than a good or service. They may not be registered under the trademark law unless they also function as trademarks or service marks by identifying the trade name user as a source of a good or service. A number of states, however, allow trade names to be registered and protected under their laws.
   B. Certification marks, such as those of Underwriters' Laboratories (the UL symbol of safety of electrical products) or the origin of a good (such as "The Wines of Bordeaux"), may function as trademarks of the issuing organization as long as the holder establishes a standard for awarding the mark and polices the standard to good effect.
   C. Collective marks are those held by a group for the use of its members. The marks of organizations such as Associated Grocers, a cooperative organization of independent businesses, or the International Brotherhood of Electrical Workers, a trade union, are treated like any other trademark by the trademark law.
   D. Trade dress, perhaps the oldest known form or trademark, consists of identifying the product of a vendor or the vendor himself or herself by visual (and sometimes auditory) cues. More on this category of marks will be presented later.

3. The Rule of "First and Continuous Use."
   Assuming that the other requirements for a mark to be classed as a trademark are met, the essential premise of common law that applies is the rule of "first and continuous use in commerce." This rule states that the individual or firm that uses a trademark first, and can demonstrate if challenged that he, she, or it was the first user of the mark and has used the mark continuously in commerce since that date, is

the owner of the mark. Marks may be claimed for use in single states or in interstate commerce.

If the validity of a mark under the "first and continuous use" rule is never tested in court, then what follows this sentence is irrelevant. If the mark is tested in court, however, the information that follows becomes very important. In a recent decision (*CreAgri, Inc. v. USNA Health Services, Inc.* (Case 05-15305, January 16, 2007)), the U.S. Ninth Circuit Court of Appeals ruled that not only must a product have been the first to use a trademark and have used it continuously since the date of first use, but its use must also have been legal. In this case, CreAgri failed to comply with the U.S. Food and Drug Administration labeling rules on a vitamin supplement product, and its trademark "Olivenol" for that product was therefore declared void.[13]

4. Other Principles Affecting the Viability of Trademarks: The Distinctiveness Requirement

After application of the "first and continuous use in commerce" rule, the other requirements for a mark to be classed as a trademark, in addition to what has gone before, are generally as follows: the mark must be "distinctive," that is, it must be capable of identifying the source of a particular good. The courts group marks into four categories, based on the relationship between the mark and the underlying product, to determine whether a particular mark is distinctive.

A. The most distinctive marks are generally construed to be those that can be called "fanciful." Such marks have no apparent descriptive relationship to the products that bear them. In the realm of words, "Xerox" and "Copal" are unrelated to the products—copying machines and camera shutters—whose trademarks they are. Such marks are inherently distinctive and are given a high degree of protection.

B. The second level of distinctiveness is possessed by those marks that are called "arbitrary." Such marks are not "made-up" words like Xerox and Copal, but are not related to the products that bear them. Thus, "Camellia" as a brand for a line of packaged dried peas and beans is arbitrary, as is "Pearl River" to identify a Chinese-made soy sauce. Neither of these choices describes the good to which it is attached, so they effectively distinguish between goods offered by the companies producing different versions of the same product. "Arbitrary" marks are considered inherently distinctive in the same way as are "fanciful" marks.

C. Marks that are "suggestive," that is, that bear a remote relationship to the goods they stand for but do not directly describe them, have substantial appeal as marketing tools because consumers create in their minds an image of the products these marks suggest, differentiating the products bearing the mark from others. If that image is positive, the product has a marketplace advantage over less suggestively named goods.

Names like Microsoft and MultiGraph suggest what the goods they represent might be, but do not directly describe them as computer hardware or software. Though suggestive marks are usually construed to be inherently distinctive, there is some risk that they may, over time, become generally recognized as descriptive of the whole class of goods of which they are members, and their status as trademarks lost. "Cellophane," a DuPont trademark, and "Thermos," a mark of American Vacuum Bottle Company, suffered this fate. Cellophane and Thermos are now generic terms descriptive of any acrylic packaging material and vacuum bottle, respectively.

D. Finally, some marks are, in fact, "descriptive" of the goods or services they represent. Stating that a vehicle is a "5.7 liter Hemi V-8" in advertising copy or even on the vehicle itself, does, in fact, describe its engine in substantial detail. Similarly, calling a cereal "All Bran" is quite specific as to its content. Such marks offer little or no protection, particularly if other vehicles have similar engines or cereals similar ingredients and a similar mark is used on these products. They are not inherently distinctive. However, a descriptive mark may acquire "secondary meaning" when the consuming public primarily associates the mark with a particular producer rather than the underling product. If this is the case, then descriptive marks may achieve protection under the law.

The vast majority of trademarks fall into the first three categories. If a trademark is not registered and its validity under the "first and continuous use" rule is never tested in the courts, whether it is or is not truly distinctive may never be determined.

Summary

Patents, copyrights, and trademarks provide intellectual property protection in different ways. To acquire a patent, the inventor of the engineering innovation or discoverer of the new scientific finding must follow a four-part sequence of verifying the novelty of the discovery or innovation, assuring that no prior application or patent exists, creating the actual patent application, and submitting the application. Each step of this process calls for rigorous adherence to procedures of the Patent Office. Acquiring a patent can be a costly process. On the other hand, a copyright exists at the moment the work to be copyrighted is completed. The date and time should be noted as evidence. No further action is called for, save creation of the existence of evidence that the work is original and was created by the "authors" who purport to have done so. Registering a copyright, which provides additional protection under the law, is significantly simpler and usually much less expensive than acquiring a patent. There is no requirement of novelty, only that the work is original and was created by those "authors" seeking protection. Registry of copyright, for example, is a precondition for filing an infringement claim in federal court. In the United States, trademark rights may be acquired in three ways: by the operation of common law, by registration in one or more of the states of the Union, or by registration with the U.S. Patent and Trademark Office.

CHAPTER 3

Development of Existing Intellectual Property Rights

The Pro-Active Stance

Patents: Ownership Does Not Guarantee Success

The ownership of a patent does not guarantee that the patented invention or discovery will be commercially successful, or even that it will find its way into production. Two most successful American scientists/inventors of the past two centuries approached the issue of using their patents in two entirely different ways. The first, Thomas Alva Edison, approached all of his many projects with the objective of producing a marketable product, in many cases with the intention of bringing that product to market himself. His approach to "advancing the engineering arts" was to start with a broad-scale commercial objective and then proceed until that objective had been achieved.

Edison's Approach to Patent Development

In this connection, Edison, working with a young physicist named Francis Upton, began his project of developing a practical incandescent lamp by examining already existing patents to see how close current technology had come to success. Realizing that a successful lamp must have a filament that would not oxidize readily and a high internal electrical resistance so it would glow, Edison used evacuated glass balls (from which as much air as possible had been removed) as his basic vessels. He then tested, in his own words, "thousands and thousands"[1] (actually over 6,000) of different filament materials until, on October 23, 1879, a carbonized cotton thread survived 13 hours of energization before failing.

This success was the genesis of Edison's patent number 223,898 of January 27, 1880, and prompted Edison to develop the concept of the electrification network, opening his first commercial generating station in New York in early 1880.[2] His system, which delivered electricity at 110 volts direct current (DC), was immediately successful, and though ultimately replaced by the more efficient-to-transmit alternating current (AC) after a long battle with George Westinghouse, the advocate of AC, it nonetheless provided the basis for electrification of the entire United States. Edison's approach to invention was a team approach. In fact, his Menlo Park facility might be classed as the first industrial research and development facility.

John M. Browning and His Patents

Another famous inventor worked in quite a different fashion from Edison. John M. Browning, a Mormon boy from Ogden, Utah, was the son of a gunsmith. John M. Browning also became a gunsmith—perhaps the most successful gunsmith in history. When Browning was a young man, all firearms were operated manually. A gun would be fired, the user would clear the action of any firing residue (usually, by this time, a cartridge case) by hand, load another round, and relock and recock the weapon in preparation for another shot. Some guns were repeaters with several rounds in a magazine, but the procedure was essentially similar for them and for single-shot weapons.

Browning spent his entire life improving the operation of firearms. In addition to designing guns that were significant improvements on most of the manual-action (i.e., person-actuated) weapons available in his time, he designed, developed, and built working prototypes of firearms that operated using their own recoil to eject fired cartridge cases, reload the weapon's chamber, recock the action, and in some cases fire the gun again and again until the shooter released the trigger. Some of his other designs used the gas generated when a gun was fired to perform the "eject, reload, recock, and repeat" firing sequence. Yet others performed all the required functions safely without having any method of locking the action except inertia.

Throughout his career, Browning remained essentially a gunsmith, in many cases being the first individual to use successfully a particular method such as recoil, gas operation, or inertia to operate a firearm. His patents were, for their day, the sine qua non of the gunsmith's art. Many of the weapons John Browning designed during his career, which lasted from 1885 to 1926, are still in production or service to this day. They include the U.S. Pistols M1911 and M1911A1 in both military and commercial versions, the Winchester Model 1894 lever-action repeating rifle, the Browning Auto-5 semi-automatic shotgun, U.S. M1919 0.30-caliber air-cooled and water-cooled machine guns, U.S. M1918 Browning Automatic Rifle (BAR), and the U.S. M2 0.50-caliber machine gun (originally the M1921). They have been manufactured by several firms, including Winchester Repeating Arms Company, Colt Patent Firearms Company, Remington Arms Company, Savage Firearms Company, and Fabrique National de Armes De Guerre of Belgium.

Edison Versus Browning: Was One Approach Better Than the Other?

How did Edison's and Browning's philosophies differ? Simply put, they chose different ways in which to develop and protect their intellectual property. When possible, Edison sought to invent something that he wanted to commercialize and then commercialized it himself. He started his own electric power company, for example, to exploit the concept of the incandescent bulb. His Edison Phonograph, both in the earlier cylinder and in later disc models, was sold by an Edison company. Edison rarely sold his patents. In his lifetime he was awarded 1,069 patents. He did not exploit a few of them, apparently seeing relatively little promise in them once he had achieved his basic objective of demonstrating the feasibility of the premise. He did exploit many others, and several of those were remarkably successful. Others, however, were not successful—but they remained his.

John Browning, on the contrary, sought to improve or create new ways of accomplishing the feat of delivering bullets accurately from a firearm with minimum of effort by the user. He received well over a hundred patents, but certainly not the over-a-thousand acquired by Edison. Most of Browning's patents, however, proved commercially successful. In this connection, Browning typically worked almost alone most of his life, obtained a "master" patent on a certain process, then licensed it to an established manufacturer, and obtained a royalty from that manufacturer in return for the use of the patent for a specified time. Browning's earlier patents were typically licensed on a lump-sum basis. He would turn the patent over to the licensee in return for a mutually agreed amount for immediate single payment. As his reputation grew, he realized that a "per-item-sold" royalty might be a better arrangement, and most of his later efforts were licensed on this basis. His only permanent assistant in his work was his son, Val Browning, who, in addition to being his father's assistant, was also an officer in the U.S. Army.

Three Ways to Develop and Protect Patents

1. Self-Commercialization of Patents

   The first way to develop one's patents is to retain and commercialize them on one's own, as did Thomas Edison. This alternative obviously calls for a certain financial capacity on the part of the patent holder. Commercializing a patent usually calls for the capacity to manufacture something—a device to make the patented product, a means of causing the patented discovery or process to occur, examples of the design for which a design patent was granted, even a way of propagating and growing patented plants. Some of these objectives can be achieved with relatively little effort, some cannot. The estimated cost of achieving these goals must be weighed against the potential revenue they will generate. To the degree to which this is possible, the decision to keep and commercialize the patent versus other alternatives may become clear.

   If one desires to keep and develop a patent, it is likely that the opportunity, perhaps even the necessity to obtain additional complementary patents, may appear. If one examines the evolution of John Browning's manually operated lever-action rifles—development of which was his only major effort that was initially based on a preexisting design—from the low-powered 1886 model through the more potent 1892, the still-in-production-today smokeless powder model 1894, and finally the definitive, truly high-powered model 1895, one sees the evolution of the mechanics of these weapons from a fairly low-powered weapon based on the black powder propellants common in the mid-1880s, through the innovative but still low-powered smokeless powder cartridges of the early 1890s, to the somewhat more powerful smokeless powders and medium-power cartridges of 1894, finally to the high-power smokeless powder cartridges available in the definitive model 1895. Each of these evolutionary steps generated additional patents for features of stronger, more sophisticated products. Thus, though all these models—the 1886, 1892, 1894, and 1895—appear similar, being activated by the effort of the shooter when the lever is worked between shots, their inner workings show substantial differences and increased strength to keep up with the developments in ammunition.

2. Licensing One's Patents to Others

One can, of course, take a second course and license a patent to another person or firm. Given the limited duration of patents, such licenses are often granted for a substantial fraction or even the total length of the patent. As was noted in the Browning case, licenses can be negotiated in at least two ways; on a lump-sum royalty basis with the royalty paid at the time the license is granted; or as a per-unit-sold royalty contract. In general, the lump-sum arrangement may be desirable if there is some doubt as to the value of the patent. If the value of the patent can be accurately appraised, then the per-unit-sold arrangement would probably be the better choice. It might even be possible to combine a lump sum with a subsequent per-unit-sold royalty agreement. It is also possible, though fairly rare, to grant nonexclusive rights to more than one licensee, but every licensee would probably insist on the specific terms of each agreement with the patent holder.

3. Outright Sale of One's Patent Inventory

The third alternative for patent development is to sell one's patent rights to another party. This implies that one cannot, for some reason, commercialize the patent oneself; that the patent, though of some value, is not sufficiently attractive to others to justify a royalty arrangement; or that, for some other reason, perhaps technological or even political, the patent's time has not come. Such a situation, if one's research agenda is consistent with one's capacities and objectives, should occur fairly seldom. It might become appropriate, however, if a patent holder perceives opportunities in another area of endeavor and seeks to raise a sum of money to finance that activity.

4. Beware the Patent Sharks

There are, of course, patent sharks that must be considered when sale rather than continued ownership of a patent seems an unwise course. Patent sharks are firms that buy patents to stockpile them, hoping to sell them to other firms that might then use them. They might also be interested in keeping the new technology represented by the patent off the market and thus out of the hands of their competitors. They usually do not reveal why they seek to purchase a patent, and thus their objectives are subject to question. In general, unless the situation is desperate and sale of the patent or patents in question is the only way to remain solvent, it is well to keep clear of such creatures. Their name "patent shark" is meaningful.

Copyrights: Their Care and Feeding; Six Ways of Getting One's Work Published

There are several alternative methods of achieving publication of a copyrighted work:

1. The first method is to produce the work under contract with an established publisher. This is the method that textbook writers and publishers most often use, the publisher contracting with an author with a known reputation and level of knowledge in the field about which the book is to be written to write the text. New writers are seldom approached to write such books, so must ordinarily approach the market using one of the other methods of securing publication. Writing texts in this manner usually recognizes that, once the text

is finished, the publisher will own the copyright and that the writer will receive royalties on its sale.

2. Submit copies of the copyrighted work to a number of established publishers, attempting to induce them to publish the work. In this case, the author usually expects to retain the copyright of the work. Though the term publication will be used here as a matter of convention, recognize that publication of a novel differs significantly in cost and expected sales volume than does publication (production) of a motion picture script. The copyright office recognizes eight types of copyrightable works. Each differs from the others, sometimes in major ways. Publication may be for an expected audience of millions of readers or for a few hundred avid collectors of a particular type of art. The value of the copyright may be low or high based on these considerations. Millions of people who read a romance novel for which they paid $7 may be less profitable to the publisher of the book than the few hundred people who buy one of the artist's signed copies or a statue by a renowned sculptor at a price of $150,000 each.

3. Works already in existence and covered by copyright are often accepted for publication on a royalty basis. The author receives a stipulated fee for each copy of the work sold. Unfortunately, unless the author has already achieved a level of fame, it is often necessary that he or she sign over the exclusive right to publication of the work to the publisher in return for the royalty compensation. This differs from alternative (A) in the sense that in this case the author has already written the book and received a copyright on it that will be signed over to the publisher as a condition of publication. In alternative (A), the terms of the contract are known before the book is written, so that the author has more power of ahead-of-time negotiation of terms than is the case in this instance.

4. If a first publication is successful, authors often find that their work will bring publication offers and royalty contracts without the need for them to sign over their exclusive right of publication to the publisher in order to successfully negotiate a royalty contract. In some instances, due to the popularity of their work, authors end up with a long-term relationship with a publishing company that may

continue for decades with the author retaining the copyrights to his or her work in return for an exclusive relationship with the publisher and royalties on books that remain in print.

5. An author may also sell his or her copyrights outright to a publisher or other interested person in order to secure cash now rather than the anticipation of money later after publication has taken place. This is a somewhat unusual approach to the management of copyrights, but if the author is unknown and has created an interesting new premise and needs cash flow, it might be an attractive alternative.

6. Finally, the alternative of self-publication may present itself. In this case, the author retains both the copyright to the work and the total amount of profit derived from the sale of his or her work. Obviously, in this situation, the cost of publication of the work will have a significant impact on the feasibility of this alternative. Such an alternative could be feasible if the author has sufficient funds to produce a motion picture cheaply and a good reputation as a producer and perhaps is even an actor who can star in his or her own production. With a good script and production values, the possibility of success is enhanced.

Trademarks: They Can Persist Longer Than Other Intellectual Property Rights and Require Different Treatment

Trademarks are meant to be used. When an individual or firm creates a trademark (or service mark), whether the mark is registered or not, the implication is that the trademark owner intends to use that trademark "in commerce." As was discussed earlier, U.S. law does not require that a trademark be registered by its proprietor in order to be validly used. Failure to register a trademark, however, may limit its protection under common law to a single state or, in an extreme instance, to a single venue.

1. Fanciful, arbitrary, and suggestive marks may seek protection under the law even if they have not yet been used in trade or commerce. Descriptive marks, however, do not qualify for protection and

therefore cannot be registered until they have acquired secondary meaning. Proof of secondary meaning is usually tested in the courts by an examination of (a) the amount and manner of advertising of the product, (b) the volume of sales of the product, (c) the length and manner of the mark's use, and (d) the results of consumer surveys.[3] (The author represented the plaintiff(s) and conducted survey research in the cases referred to in note 30. Secondary meaning on the basis of the survey research was found to exist in both cases.)

2. The merits of registering a trademark are several (see 15 USC 1051). In addition to conferring on the registrant the right to use the trademark nationally, subject to a few minor restrictions (15 USC 1072), registration also gives notice to others that the trademark is owned by the registrant and enables the registrant to bring an infringement suit in federal court (15 USC 1121). In the event of a finding of infringement, the plaintiff may be allowed to recover treble damages, attorneys' fees, and other remedies. After 5 years, registered trademarks can become incontestable, at which time the registrant's exclusive right to use the mark is conclusively established.

3. The Patent and Trademark Office (PTO) is the federal agency for approval of trademark applications. The PTO can reject an application for a number of reasons (15 USC 1052). Perhaps the most common reason for rejection is a finding that a descriptive mark has not achieved secondary meaning. "Immoral or scandalous" marks can also be rejected, as can marks that are primarily surnames and marks that are likely to cause confusion with existing marks. Rejection of the application for registration does not, however, mean that the mark is not entitled to trademark protection, only that the mark does not receive the benefits noted in the above paragraph on the merits of registration (15 USC 1125).

4. Trademarks, just as patents and copyrights, can be held and developed by the trademark owner for his or her own uses; they may also be licensed for use by another (this is sometimes called franchising) for a specific period of time or under specific conditions of compliance; or they may be sold for use by another, who becomes the new trademark holder.

The Duration of Trademarks

Trademarks remain in effect as long as the product(s) covered by the trademark are offered in the marketplace by a legal holder or licensee of the mark. In this respect, trademarks differ from the other forms of intellectual property rights supported by government, patents, and copyrights, all of which have finite duration.

Loss of Trademark Rights

There are several ways in which trademark rights may be lost. Some of these are intentional while others grow out of error or misfeasance on the part of the trademark holder. A trademark is abandoned when its proprietor discontinues its use with no intention to resume its use at a later date. This intent can be inferred from the circumstances. Nonuse for a period of 3 years constitutes prima facie evidence of intent to abandon a mark. The fact that trademarks have no usual limits on their duration is based on the premise that they are being used and trademark owners are not entitled to stockpile potentially useful marks. The Los Angeles Dodgers, for example, lost the rights to the Brooklyn Dodgers trademark through abandonment, despite their claims to the contrary, in the early 1990s.[4]

If a trademark is improperly licensed or assigned, it may be lost. The use of a trademark that is franchised, for example, must be subject to adequate quality control and supervision or the trademark will be canceled. If a trademark holder assigns the rights to his or her mark to another without a corresponding sale of related assets, it will similarly be canceled. The logic behind this action is that a trademark disposed of in this fashion no longer serves the purpose of identifying the goods of a particular provider (the original trademark owner).[5]

It is also possible to lose the exclusive rights to one's trademark if the trademark becomes generic. A trademark can become generic if, usually over a number of years, it has become, in the minds of a substantial majority of the public, the name by which a general category of goods has become known, not just the products of a specific provider. A number of well-known trademarks have suffered this fate. In addition to the marks "Cellophane" and "Thermos," "Aspirin" and "Shredded Wheat" were originally marks that subsequently became generic.

Summary

Merely having acquired protection for one's intellectual property does not imply that one will be successful in developing that property. Thomas Edison and John Browning were two successful inventors working toward the end of the nineteenth century and beginning of the twentieth. Their approaches to invention were quite different. Edison employed a large staff to achieve his objectives and often manufactured his own inventions. Browning usually worked alone or with a very small staff, and more often licensed his patents to governments or large firms that manufactured guns. Both approaches were consistent with the views of their holder—both of whom were successful. There are three ways to develop patents. First, one may develop them oneself; second, one may license one's patents to others; and third, one can sell one's patents outright. There are six ways to develop copyrights, involving when and how the work will be or has been produced, the fame of the author, the method of payment for the work, and so forth. Because trademarks are meant to be used, they usually remain the property of the original owner. There is no statutory limit to the duration of a trademark, so consideration must be given to the issue of for how long a particular trademark might persist. If a mark is used continuously, it is unlikely that it will be lost to its proprietor. If use is suspended, the trademark may be lost to its owner.

PART II

Active Protection of Intellectual Property Rights From Infringement

Conditions of Infringement and Defense

CHAPTER 4

Patents

How They Can Be Infringed and Should Be Defended

The Concept of the Master Patent

The right to a properly patented invention or discovery is *absolute* during the term of the patent. No one other than the patent holder can exercise rights of use, sale, license, or other commercialization of the patented concept during that period. If the patent is sold or otherwise permanently transferred to a new owner, he or she becomes the patent holder. The previous chapter referred to the importance of a "master" patent in the case of John M. Browning's patents. In effect, a "master" patent is one that is so comprehensive of the scientific or engineering principle or an array of principles claimed in the patent that it is impossible to achieve the desired objective without using the methods claimed by the patent. Master patents are rare. They typically appear early in the history of the scientific examination of a particular process or in the design of engineering methods and subsequent developments depend heavily on them. In such a case, the patent is self-protecting, in the sense that the efforts of others to avoid use of the patented processes will either fail or result in an infringement. There were many efforts, often by talented engineers, to improve on or avoid the use of Browning's patents. The results of their work were often simply failures, such as the Winchester Model 1911 automatic shotgun, designed by Thomas C. Johnson, a very competent engineer, specifically to avoid Browning's patents. Johnson is quoted as having said that it took him "nearly ten years to design a gun that did not infringe on Browning's design."[1] Truly, Johnson's design did not infringe on Browning's patent. It was also, however, inherently awkward and dangerous to use and was a failure in the marketplace. Other attempts to avoid Browning's patents led to more successful but awkward weapons such as the Luger auto-loading pistol and the Pedersen semi-automatic rifle, both of which used a modified flip-up recoil action using a toggle. They worked, but took up more room than weapons based on Browning's designs.

What If You Do Not Have a Master Patent?

Patents with a less-than-master basis: Most patents filed these days are based on "improvements" on master patents granted a number of years ago. As such, their value is usually substantially lesser than a master patent. They do have value, but that value is often based on getting the products that use the improvement into production as soon as possible so that revenue can be generated before another improvement renders the present improvement useless. Since the opening of the U.S. Patent Office in 1836, nearly 8 million patents have been granted. In 2010, 520,277 patent applications were filed and 244,341 patents were granted. During 2001–2010, 3,841,790 patent applications were filed and 1,895,168 patents were granted.[2] Obviously, relatively few of the almost 2 million patents granted during the past decade are "master" patents. Thus, the real (useful) average duration of the patent granted today must be substantially less than 20 years provided by law. Recognition of this fact may have a substantial effect on the decision made by the patent holder as to what to do in the event of an apparent infringement.

What Makes for a Patent Infringement?

As a particular point of law, Title 35 Part 271 of the U.S. Code (35 USC 271) states that infringement occurs "whenever anyone who does not possess the authority to do so makes, uses, offers to sell, or sells any patented invention within the United States or imports into the United States any patented invention during the term of the patent." In addition, anyone who actively induces infringement is also liable as an infringer. Anyone who sells or offers to sell in the United States a component of a patented machine, or who manufactures, combines, or composes, or otherwise creates a material or apparatus or apparatus for use in practicing a patented process, constituting a material part of the invention, knowing the same to be especially made or adapted for use in infringement of the patent, and NOT a staple article or commodity of commerce suitable for a substantial noninfringing use, shall be liable as a contributory infringer.

Conversely, an American firm that supplies, or causes to be supplied, the fundamental components of a patented invention to a foreign firm for the purpose of reproducing the invention is also liable as an infringer.

Specific Reactions to Apparent Infringement— Patent Enforcement

A. It is the function of the Patent Office to grant patents upon proof by applicants that the invention or discovery for which they are asking a patent is valid. It is the patent holder's responsibility, upon becoming aware of an infringement, to take those actions appropriate to mount a defense against the infringement. Infringement of a patent consists specifically of a violation of the terms of the patent granted to the patent holder. These terms have been explained at length in earlier sections. It is the responsibility of the patent holder to state and prove that the alleged infringer has illicitly used the invention or discovery covered by the patent.

B. Patent holders have the option, should they so desire, of contacting the infringer of their patent and attempting to negotiate an amicable arrangement to license the patent. Such attempts are sometimes successful, and the resulting license is referred to in the language of the patent courts as a "carrot license" (referring to the carrot and stick analogy). If a license is granted as the result of a patent infringement lawsuit or the threat of such a suit, it is called a "stick license."

C. If a patent holder is not practicing his or her patent, that is, if he or she is not using the patented invention to produce a product or service, then he or she is known as a "nonpracticing entity," and the courts have ruled that a nonpracticing entity cannot receive injunctive relief. That is, the courts will not issue an injunction forcing the patent infringer to cease and desist using the patent. A practicing patent holder may receive injunctive relief, but it is a lengthy and costly process. The preferable remedy for enforcement available to most patent holders is to secure compensation for the use of their patent.

D. The ultimate enforcement action related to the infringement of a patent is to sue the infringer. Patent infringement suits are filed in the appropriate court of federal jurisdiction. The patent holder may ask the court for an injunction to prevent the continuation of the patent infringement and may also ask the court for an award of damages resulting from the infringement.

The defendant in a patent infringement suit may raise the question of the validity of the patent he or she is alleged to have infringed. The court then decides on the question. The defendant may also claim that his or her actions do not constitute infringement. Infringement, as should be recalled, is determined by the language of the claims of the patent and if the defendant's product does not fall within the scope of the language of any of the claims in the patent, there is no literal infringement.

E. The rules of procedure of the federal courts allow for appeals of the decisions of the district courts to the Court of Appeals of that Federal Circuit. The Supreme Court of the United States may subsequently take a case on a writ of certiorari. If the U.S. Government infringes a patent, the patent holder may seek damages in the U.S. Court of Federal Claims. By right of eminent domain, the government may use any patented invention without permission from the patent holder, but must compensate the patent holder for use of his or her patent by the government.

F. Needless to say, litigating a patent infringement suit is lengthy and can be quite an expensive process. Richard D. Margiano, in the article "Cost and Duration of Patent Litigation," *Managing Intellectual Property*, February 1, 2009, states an average cost of a patent litigation of "about $3 million," with an appeal adding some "$2 million." He estimates the time expended for an average trial to be 2 years, with the appeal increasing that up to 3 years.[3] Margiano cites six major factors that affect the cost of litigation to a client. These are: (a) the product's value to your business, (b) the product's value to your adversary and their resources, (c) the number of patents, defenses, and parties involved, (d) the volume of evidence, (e) the venue—different courts behave differently, and (f) the law firm and the litigation strategy adopted.

Summary

Patent rights are absolute during the term of the patent. The initial patent holder can use, sell, license, or otherwise commercialize the patent. Possessing a "master patent" effectively makes the holder of that patent a complete monopolist over the scientific and engineering principles claimed by the patent for the duration of the patent. Master patents are rare. Most patents today are "improvements," sometimes trivial ones, on existing patents, and of much less value than the masters. They do have value, however, and are subject to infringement. Infringement of a patent occurs when anyone who does not possess the authority to do so acts as though he or she was the patent holder. In the event that a patent holder discovers what he or she perceives to be an infringement of his or her patent, several options present themselves. They may attempt to negotiate a license with the infringer, seek injunctive relief against the infringer (a seldom successful alternative), or sue in federal court for a cessation of the infringement and compensatory damages. Because the alleged infringer can question the validity of the patent in the same court, a patent infringement suit is often a lengthy and expensive process, often costing millions of dollars. One must weigh this cost against the possible reward for success and proceed accordingly.

CHAPTER 5

Copyrights: The Current U.S. Copyright Law and Its Provisions

Coverages and Exemptions

Changes in Copyright Coverage Have Come Thick and Fast in Recent Years

1. The amendments to the U.S. Copyright Law (17 USC 101 et seq.) that have been implemented since 1976 extended copyright protection to creative works beginning at the moment of their creation. They also extended copyright protection to recorded works such as motion pictures and recording of specific performances of pieces of music. In 1998, the Digital Millenium Copyright Act (DMCA) amended Section 104 of 17 USC to provide protection for computer programs against infringement. The owner of a work covered by the DMCA that is copied or used without the permission of the copyright owner, even though that program does not meet the traditional requirements for a "tangible medium of expression," can sue for copyright infringement. This aspect of copyright can cut both ways. Authors, artists, photographers, sculptors, journalists, mapmakers, computer programmers, and creators of all other "original works of authorship fixed in a tangible medium of expression" covered by the new meaning of that term must be aware of their rights and of the rights of similar persons so they can avoid accidentally infringing on the work of others and protect their own work from infringement.

2. There is no specific demand for "novelty" in creating a copyrightable "creative work." The essence of a copyright claim is that the creator of the work has created the particular version of the thing for which copyright is claimed. Some things cannot be copyrighted, among them being facts. Facts owe their existence to the conditions that created them. The occurrence of a hurricane is a fact. An author who writes a book about a hurricane cannot copyright the existence of the hurricane, thus preventing others from writing about it. If he or she were, however, to write a narrative about that hurricane, his or her style of writing, choice of words, and their arrangement and order of presentation could be copyrighted. Videotapes of news events subsequently licensed to broadcast stations by the original compiler remain, in their "raw" (unedited) form, the copyrighted property of the compiler.[1] Assuming, then, that one is aware that one has a copyright over certain work, the question of protecting that right becomes important. One can "stake one's claim" in a visible sense by assuring that persons who come into possession of the protected work are provided with a copyright claim notice appended to the work as was mentioned before. Such a notice may act as a deterrent to someone who might copy the work were such a notice not provided. At the worst, it provides due notice that such a claim has been made.

3. In general, a copyright granted under the current copyright law of the United States (17 USC 101 et seq.) conveys exclusive rights to the matter copyrighted to the copyright owner. There are, however, a number of limitations on those exclusive rights, which will be briefly enumerated and explained here.

The exemptions to exclusive use of copyrighted materials include, in general, the following:

A. "Right to Fair Use" (17 USC 107): The first limitation on the exclusive rights of copyright holders is the "right to fair use" by others for purposes of criticism, comment, news reporting, teaching (including multiple copies for classroom use), scholarship, or research; such fair use in a particular case is determined by the purpose and character of the use, the nature of the copyrighted work, the amount and substantiality of the portion used in relation to the copyrighted work as a whole, and the effect of the use on the potential market for or value of the copyrighted work.

B. "Right to Make Multiple Archive Copies" (17 USC 108): It is not an infringement of copyright for a library or archive, or any of its employees acting in the scope of their employment, to produce no more than one copy of a work: (i) if the purpose of the copy is noncommercial, (ii) the collections of the library are open to the public or to relevant researchers in a specialized field, and (iii) the reproduction includes a notice of copyright or a notice that copyright exists even if no such notice appeared on the original document.

Additional conditions pertaining to library copies are stated in the law for works in the process of preservation or for security and for certain other conditions. In addition, copying and distribution of musical, pictorial, graphic, or sculptured work, or motion pictures or other audiovisual works except those made for news purposes is not permitted.

C. "Freedom to Dispose of Private Property" (17 USC 109): In general, owners in due course of a particular copy or phonorecord lawfully made under this title may sell or otherwise dispose of their copy of the work without permission from the copyright owners. Special conditions apply when disposition of recordings of musical works, copies of computer programs, and certain other works are made for commercial gain.

D. "Exemption of Educational Performances from Accusation of Infringement" (17 USC 110): This section of the act exempts performances and displays of copyrighted works for a number of educational purposes from accusation of infringement of copyright by virtue of these performances and displays.

E. "Right to Produce Certain Retransmissions on Radio and TV" (17 USC 111): Secondary transmission (i.e., retransmission of radio and television signals formerly broadcast by a duly licensed radio or television station) and the provision of technology and equipment to facilitate such transmissions does not constitute infringement of copyright under a broad array of conditions stated in this section of the law.

F. "Right to Retransmit of Ephemeral Recordings" (17 USC 112): In effect, this section allows a duly licensed radio or television station to make an "ephemeral recording," that is, a digital copy, of a performance it has transmitted live for its own use and retransmit that performance for a period of not more than 6 months after the original transmission without being guilty of copyright infringement. This section also lists a number of other conditions that affect "ephemeral recordings" and their use and retention.

G. "Right to Copy Computer Programs under Certain Conditions" (17 USC 117): The owner of a computer program may make or authorize the making of another copy or adaptation of that program so long as (i) the copying or adaptation is a necessary step in the use of the program in a machine and for no other use and (ii) the new copy is for archival purposes and is destroyed when possession of an archival copy would no longer be lawful.

H. "Right to Certain Actions of Superstations and Network Stations" (17 USC 119): This complex section of the law covers the operations of "superstations and network stations" and details the actions that must be taken to assure that station licenses and operational characteristics comply with Federal Communications Commission (FCC) regulations and thereby bring the station into compliance with rules that prevent infringing broadcasts.

I. "Exemption of Reproduction of Phonorecords for the Disabled" (17 USC 121): Reproduction and distribution of phonorecords of a previously published, nondramatic literary work is not infringement if the phonorecords are in special formats exclusively for the use of the blind or other persons with disabilities.

J. "Exemption of Secondary Transmissions by Satellites for Broadcast" (17 USC 122): This rather complex provision of the law stipulates the conditions that must apply if a satellite carrier is to legally produce secondary transmissions of those by a broadcast station in a local market.

Of these limitations listed, the most important is the first, simply because "fair use" occurs so often in the course of daily events. Verbatim quotes of written work form the very basis of editorial criticism and comment and are often the essence of news reporting. To deny the press the ability to report current events because certain aspects of those events may have been recorded in copyrighted documents is unfair, and it is this that the law recognizes. Note, however, that the limitation does not cover the use of entire documents or even sections of documents willy-nilly, but only under certain conditions and to a limited degree.

Perhaps the best way to state the effect of these limitations would be to say that the law, while granting them, also limits their scope.

Resisting Infringement: Enforcement of Copyrights Is the Owner's Responsibility

1. Infringement of a copyright is, for the most part, an act involving reproduction and distribution of copies of the copyrighted work. Since the law requires that the original work be "tangible," so must most infringements be tangible.

2. The responsibility for protecting copyrights lies with the copyright owner. The Copyright Office simply registers claims of copyright, but does not enforce infringement claims. As a first effort, the copyright owner who has evidence that his or her copyright has been infringed can elect to approach the alleged infringer and attempt to negotiate an amicable settlement of the matter. It is conceivable that an infringer who has infringed unintentionally might agree to such an arrangement.

3. The second action available to the copyright owner is to file suit against the alleged infringer. Such a suit can be filed in any federal court at the appropriate level of jurisdiction (typically the district court with authority over the domicile of the plaintiff). The logic behind this flexibility of venue lies in the mobility of things that bear copyrights. A book, for example, is typically offered for sale at least regionally, if not nationally, so bringing suit in a state court, given that such a court can only grant damages that can be collected against the defendant's assets in that state, is ineffective.

4. In the course of pressing his or her suit, the copyright owner may have to demonstrate that he or she has properly claimed the copyright he or she seeks to defend. Since registration is not required to claim the protection of copyright, the date on which the work was completed must be irrefutably documented in some fashion. In addition, the alleged infringer may cast doubt on the originality of the subject work. This is a more insubstantial claim because language, art, and the other bases of work on which copyrights may be granted are flexible and must be taken in context. Thus, the phrase "I am a man" in one context is simply a statement of fact, yet in another might be a central part of a deep philosophical discourse.[2] In the prior context, "I am a man" would be uncopyrightable as a mere statement of fact. In the context of Dickens' novel, *A Tale of Two Cities*, it is central to the dialogue between the character Stryver and the other character, Sydney Carton. Stryver is a successful attorney, but Carton writes all his briefs and is the brain behind his success. Stryver, nonetheless, is the one who makes the philosophical claim to manhood.

5. Assuming that the right to the copyright has been demonstrated, the infringement may be determined by the body of evidence that must first include proof that the material alleged to be infringing was copied from the copyrighted work. Then it must be determined that the copied material is not covered by any of the various limitations on the exclusive rights conferred by the copyright. If the copied work is not so limited, then an infringement has occurred.

Chapter 5 of 17 USC Provides for Several Remedies for Infringement of Copyright

1. (17 USC 502) The court of civil jurisdiction of an action arising under the copyright law may grant temporary and final injunctions against an infringer on such terms as it deems reasonable to prevent or restrain infringement of a copyright

2. (17 USC 503) At any time while an action under the copyright law is pending, the court may order the impounding, on such terms as seem reasonable, of

A.   all copies or phonorecords claimed to have been made or used in violation of the exclusive right of the copyright holder;

B.   all plates, molds, matrices, masters, tapes, film negatives, or other articles by which such copies of phonorecords may be reproduced;

C.   records documenting the manufacture, sale, or receipt of things involved in any such violation of the copyright law, provided that any records so seized shall be taken into the custody of the court.

If impoundment covered in these terms is undertaken, the law calls upon the court to enter a protective order with respect to discovery or use of the records or information that have been impounded, requiring that disclosure of confidential, private, proprietary, or privileged information is not improperly made. It further states that, as part of a final judgment or decree, the court may order the destruction or other reasonable disposition of all the things being subject to impoundment.

3. (17 USC 504) In general, persons found guilty of infringement of a copyright are liable to one or the other of (a) the copyright owner's actual damages and any additional profits of the infringer or (b) statutory damages as provided in the law. The copyright owner is required to prove only the infringer's gross revenues, while the infringer must prove his or her deductible expenses and the elements of profit derived from sources other than the copyrighted work.

Depending on the specific conditions of the case, statutory damages may be as little as $200 or as much as $150,000 per offense. The court has considerable discretion as to the specific amount of damages it awards to the copyright owner that proves willful infringement by the infringer, up to the $150,000 limit. Unless they can prove otherwise, infringers are assumed to have acted willfully. If an infringer can prove that his or her infringement was not willful, the court may choose to levy a damage award of as little as $200 to the copyright holder.

4. (17 USC 505) The law provides for full recovery, at the discretion of the court, of full costs by or against anyone other than the

United States or any officer of the United States. Reasonable attorney's fees may be awarded to the prevailing party as part of the costs.

5. (17 USC 506) A willful infringement may become a criminal offense under 18 USC 2319 if the infringement was committed (a) for commercial advantage or private financial gain; (b) by the reproduction or distribution, including electronically, of one or more copies of any copyrighted work during any 180-day period having a total value of more than $1,000; or (c) unauthorized distribution of a work being prepared for commercial distribution on a computer network accessible to members of the public if the unauthorized distributor knew or should have known that the work was intended for commercial distribution.

6. (17 USC 507) In general, criminal proceedings under this title must be commenced within 5 years after the alleged infringement began. Similarly, civil actions under this title must be commenced within 3 years of the beginning of the alleged infringement.

7. (17 USC 511) The immunity from prosecution under their own laws ordinarily held by the United States, its officers, and the several states and their officers is waived by the terms of the copyright law. Any entity or person so described can be sued in the federal courts and, if found guilty, be subject to any of the penalties provided for any other infringer in such courts.

8. Materials in other sections of the law (17 USC 508, 510, 512, 513) deal with application of the copyright law to material held, stored, and distributed online or in cable distribution systems. It is highly technical and should be reviewed, in the event of necessity, by persons with suitable engineering and legal expertise to speak to the issues in the specific case.

Summary

Since 1976, creative works receive copyright protection beginning at the moment of their creation. The 1976 amendment of the Lanham Act also extended copyright protection to motion pictures and recordings of specific performances of musical selections. Computer programs are now also protected under the Digital Millenium Copyright Act of 1998.

In general, a copyright granted under the current copyright law grants exclusive rights to the copyright owner. There are, however, a number of exemptions to these rights, found in 17 USC 107 through 112 and 17 USC 117, 119, 121, and 122. Of these, the most important is 17 USC 107, the "Right to Fair Use." The responsibility for protecting copyrights lies with the copyright owner. The copyright owner may attempt to settle amicably with the alleged infringer. If this fails, suit may be filed in an appropriate federal court. Since registration is no longer mandatory to claim copyright, the copyright holder should be prepared to prove that he or she has properly claimed the right. If the claim is upheld, the court may apply any of a number of remedies provided under Section 5 of USC 17.

CHAPTER 6

Trademark Infringement: Protecting the Oldest and Most Rapidly Changing of Intellectual Property Classes

Trademarks: Cases of Direct Infringement in the Era of High Rate of Technological Evolution

The law with respect to trademarks, service marks, and the like within the United States differs from the law that bears on patents and copyrights, in that three levels of protection for trademarks are available: protection by common law, by state statute, and by federal law. The existence of these three levels of protection makes for a more complicated array of possibilities in terms of the jurisdiction of the courts in a given case, as well as the degree of protection afforded to trademark holders.

Trademarks: Eligible for Three Levels of Legal Protection

A. Protection under Common Law

Protection under common law is generally considered to be the weakest form because the protection it provides may be geographically limited to the goods or services protected and to the relief available in the event of a finding of infringement.

B. Protection Offered Under State law

Protection provided by state statute may be quite strong—within the state where that statute is the law. This obviously is a significant geographical limitation on protection from infringement.

Note that the ᵀᴹ or ˢᴹ mark may be used in connection with any appropriate trade- or service mark. They are often used by products protected by common or state law.

C. Protection Available Under Federal Law

Finally, a trademark protected in the Principal Register of Marks at the federal level receives the highest level of protection, followed by a mark enrolled in the Supplemental Register. Both of these can bear the ® symbol indicating their high level of protection.

There are, however, differences between the levels of protection offered by registration in the Principal Register and the Supplemental Register. Those differences lie in the area of distinctiveness. Marks that are fanciful, arbitrary, or suggestive may seek registration in the Principal Register on the premise of inherent distinctiveness even if they have not yet been used in trade or commerce.

Descriptive marks, inclusive of geographic terms, and surnames, however, do not qualify the products that bear them for application for registration in the Principal Register until they have acquired secondary meaning. Secondary meaning occurs when a trademark comes to be synonymous with the source of the product or service that bears it, that is, when consumers identify the product with the trademark. Proof of secondary meaning is usually tested in the courts by an examination of (a) the amount and manner of advertising of the product, (b) the volume of sales of the product, (c) the length and manner of the mark's use, and (d) the results of consumer surveys.

Being in the Supplemental Register does confer some benefits on the mark. Marks registered in this register can be the basis for a federal lawsuit, registry of the mark can serve as the basis for application for international trademark status, and registration in the Supplemental Register blocks applied-for marks that are similar to the registered mark.

There can be no opposition proceeding to contest the registration of a mark in the Supplemental Register. Supplemental marks are never published so that if someone wishes to petition for removal of such a mark, they must wait for a cancellation proceeding. If a mark in the Supplemental Register achieves movement to the Principal Register by filing a new application, however, then the mark will be published and opposition becomes possible.

Appropriate Action if Infringement Is Apparent

In a case of apparent infringement, deciding on appropriate action can be difficult, not only because of the different levels of protection involved, but also because of the different types of infringement. It is always possible for the victim of apparent infringement to approach the alleged infringer on discovering the infringement, point out the nature of the infringement, and negotiate a settlement. This might even be the best course in the event that the infringer was ignorant of the infringement due to geographical separation of the parties or to other factors that led the infringer to be unaware of the existence of the offended party.

Methods for Acting Against a Direct Infringer if Negotiation Fails

The next course for the infringed party, assuming a negotiated settlement cannot be arranged, is to file suit against the infringer in the appropriate jurisdiction. Under common law, the usual move would be to file suit in a court in the domicile of the infringer so as to have access to the infringer's assets in the event of a judgment against him.

Acting on the assumption that a particular trademark consists of a graphic depiction of some sort (often called a "logo") and a name, together the most common form of trademark, direct infringement would occur if a potential competitor used an exact or a nearly exact mark in connection with the same class of product (or service). Trade dress, though not exactly meeting the terms of the above definition, is nevertheless treated the same as a "usual" trademark, especially when it is federally registered. Given that the basis of the concept of trademark protection is that the trademark owner must possess a distinctive or protectable symbol and that the infringer's action must have created the likelihood of consumer confusion between the two products, firms, or concepts, the identity between the two marks would leave little doubt that the junior latter user's (the newer) mark caused confusion with the senior user's former (the older) mark on the part of the public. If neither of the parties to the situation has registered their mark at the state or federal level, then rules of common law apply and the proof of seniority and the obvious likelihood of confusion on the part of consumers should provide sufficient evidence of infringement to bring forth a judgment in favor of the senior mark holder. If the offending party's actions were inadvertent, that is, they were unaware of the existence of the senior mark holder, the judgment might be in the form of an injunction requiring the abandonment of the infringing mark with or without the payment of monetary damages.

As long as a trademark owner does not become aware of the existence of a competitor using the same trademark, it is unlikely that an action for infringement will be filed. It is, of course, more likely that the mark owner will become aware of infringement if the infringer becomes sufficiently large to be considered an actual competitor. Assuming that both parties, the infringer and the victim of infringement, reside in the same state, the usual course would be for the offended trademark owner to file suit in a state court under the state's trademark registration law or Unfair Trade Practices Act or, as appropriate. The trademark registration law of the state would have effect if either or both of the parties had registered their trademarks with the state. All the states have Unfair Trade Practices Acts or laws with similar names and content, which, in effect, require businesses to "play fair" in their activities in the marketplace. These laws would apply if unregistered trademarks were involved in an infringement dispute.

The mechanism for legal action in direct infringement cases varies with the status of the parties. If negotiation with an inadvertent infringer fails, the alternative usually involves litigation. If the firm or individual whose mark was infringed upon has or has not registered it in their home state, regardless of the registration of the infringer, suit should be filed in the appropriate court in the home state of the infringer. If the infringer is known to have a presence (do business or offer to do business) in more than one state, filing actions in all those states is often wise. The only situation in which an action for infringement should be filed otherwise would be if the infringed firm's trademark was federally registered, in which instance the case could be filed in federal court, but still ordinarily in the domicile (or in all those places where the infringer has a presence) of the accused infringer. Thereafter, the normal procedures for a civil litigation on a tort (an injury to the plaintiff not involving a breach of contract) would proceed.

Trademark Piracy: A Creature of the New Technologies

Trademark pirates are individuals or companies, often located in developing countries, that monitor applications for trademark registrations in similar countries by large foreign companies and immediately register those trademarks in their own or nearby countries. Then, when the large foreign firms seek to enter their country, the local mark holders demand that the foreign firms abandon their effort to enter the pirate's country or pay extortionate fees to acquire their own mark, or even demand that the pirate be made a joint-venture partner to the firm that owns the trademark legitimately in other countries. The only real remedy against such behavior is for a firm that is expanding in the global market to carefully investigate the trademark records in countries that they are considering entering and, if they find their mark already registered there, reconsider the entry. If their mark is not registered in the suspect pirate's country entering that country might remain a possibility.

Trademarks: Cases of *Indirect* Infringement

1. Creation of a New Type of Trademark Protection as the Federal Government Recognizes the Concept of Trademark Dilution
   Until 1995, the defining law applied to the registration and claiming of trademark rights in the United States was the Lanham Act of 1946 as variously amended (15 USC 1125 et seq.). The law provided for preservation of trademark rights at the federal level through two methods: (a) proof of first and continuous use of the claimed mark (a common law approach) and (b) registry with the trademark office (a statutory approach). It supplemented the trademark laws of the states, many of which provided greater

protection for marks registered in their state than did the Lanham Act nationally, particularly when indirect competition was involved. Registry with the trademark office provided prima facie evidence of first use to the registrant, the ultimate burden of proof of any claim for infringement resting with the registrant, who was typically the plaintiff in a civil suit concerning the matter. Registration of a trademark thus provided evidentiary coverage of the registrant's right to trademark ownership and some protection of the mark against infringement even if first and continuous use could not be proven. The Lanham Act was reasonably effective in providing causes of action for trademark holders against direct infringement.

2. The Trademark Holder Must Initiate Action in Any Infringement Case

Under normal circumstances of direct infringement, trademark owners were protected against infringement of their trademark by competitors as long as they could demonstrate first use of the mark. In the event of perceived infringement, it was the responsibility of the trademark owner to sue the purported infringer in a court of appropriate venue, alleging the infringement and providing proof of its occurrence. The underlying conception of what constitutes direct trademark infringement is twofold: (a) the trademark owner must first possess a distinctive or protectable symbol and (b) the alleged infringer's action must have created likelihood of confusion among consumers between the two products, firms, or concepts. In the majority of cases, the firms and products involved in trademark infringement actions would be direct competitors—that is, the products involved were direct substitutes for each other.

3. Direct Infringement, When Discovered Is Usually Obvious

In such cases, confusion on the part of consumers between the two products was usually very damaging to the trademark owner. Having one's differentiating mark "pirated" makes null and void the strategy that argued for creating it in the first place.

A. Prior to 1995, only direct infringement fell under the purview of federal law

There was a distinct area of trademark law evident in statute and litigation in almost half of the number of states of the United States since at least the late nineteenth century that remained "fuzzy" in its interpretation and application at the federal level. This was the area of trademark dilution.

B. An operant definition of trademark dilution

For purposes of discussion, dilution of a trademark may be said to occur when the action of someone who is *not* the trademark owner results in a loss of value of the trademark to the owner without confusion on the part of consumers. The earliest case on record related to trademark dilution grew out of the introduction of a line of bicycles christened "Kodak Bicycles" into the U.S. market in the late 1890s. The Eastman firm, proprietors of the trademark "Kodak" for photographic goods, brought suit against the Kodak Cycle Company and prevailed[1] upon the court holding that, despite the complete lack of likelihood of confusion between the two products, the Kodak mark should be protected against the harm it might suffer by being used as a name for bicycles.

C. The federal government remains disinterested

Even after the Kodak case, the federal Congress was subsequently content to leave issues of dilution up to the courts to litigate on a case-by-case basis. During the course of the twentieth century, however, about half of the states of the American Union passed trademark dilution statutes. Needless to say, these statutes were not identical, nor were they applied or interpreted the same way, but they did exist.

New Legislation Enters the Scene: The Trademark Dilution Act of 1995

1. Matters of dealing with trademark dilution remained in the hands of the individual states until 1995, when Congress passed the Trademark Dilution Act. An amendment to the Lanham Act (15 USC 1125, Sec. 43), the new law prohibited the use of a famous trademark by a third party that caused dilution of the distinctive quality of the

mark, that is, reduction of its value to its proprietor. Based on the trademark dilution concepts advanced by Frank Schechter in 1927, the underlying logic was that the public derived benefit from protection of the famous mark and that reduction of the value of such a mark by an interloper was wrong, even if the public was free from confusion.[2]

2. The 1995 Act defined trademark dilution for the purpose of the law as "the lessening of the capacity of a famous mark to identify and distinguish goods or services, regardless of the presence or absence of competition between the owner of a famous mark and other parties or likelihood of confusion, mistake, or deception" (15 USC 1127, Sec. 47) arising out of their use thereof. This definition did not obstruct existing state laws. Many of the existing state statutes go further than did the 1995 federal statute, waiving, for example, the requirement that a mark be "famous" to be protected against dilution.

3. Fame of a mark and the likelihood of dilution: The issue of the "fame" of a mark calls for some discussion. Having used the term in its definition of dilution for purposes of the 1995 Act, the Congress suggested eight factors that might be used as criteria by which "fame" might be measured. These were:

   A. duration (of time) and extent of use of the mark;
   B. duration and extent of advertising of the mark;
   C. size of the geographic area in which the mark had been used;
   D. degree to which the mark was "distinctive"—either because of the mark itself or through acquisition of the characteristic;
   E. degree to which the mark was recognized;
   F. method—the channels of trade—by which the product is or was distributed or marketed;
   G. use of the mark by third parties; and
   H. whether the mark was federally registered.

There is obviously some area for debate as to the meaning of these criteria. What, for example, constitutes sufficient duration of use or of advertising to create fame? How large, geographically, must be the extent of distribution of the mark to establish its fame? And, perhaps most interesting of all, what constitutes "distinctiveness" and how much of that must be present for dilution to occur?

It is beyond the scope of this text to explore at length the process of quantification that might be applied to each of the above criteria, which is perhaps why the criteria were used. Nonetheless, it can be suggested that certain broad conceptual rules apply. One such might be that "confected" marks, through their inherent uniqueness, would have an easier task of proving fame than marks composed of preexistent words or syllables. Harking back to the first mention of dilution in this document, the name KODAK, a completely confected term, makes an excellent example of the case for a distinctive mark. More recent confected marks such as VERIZON, CYBEX, and FUBU and foreign marks unfamiliar to Americans such as KUBOTA and DAEWOO fill that bill. However, how distinctive are marks such as Best Western, Best Buy, and Best Products? The 1995 Act remains mute on that point. As will be noted later, the new 2006 Act changes the criteria for fame significantly.

4. The Public Policy Component of the 1995 Act: Recalling that the original basis for U.S. trademark law was to protect the public from fraud and deception, a strong cause of action, the justification for a dilution statute is significantly weaker. It grows out of acknowledgment of the premise that trademark claimants should derive a benefit from their claim regardless of a lack on the part of the public of confusion regarding the identity of the mark's proprietor. Dilution does not require confusion for its likelihood. It is for this reason that there was a tendency, even before the passage of the 1995 Act, to add a dilution claim to all trademark litigations in states that had dilution laws. Thus, if the trademark claim failed, dilution still remained as a basis for injunctive relief.[3]

The passage of the federal dilution law, according to some, including members of the federal bench, threatened to submerge the preexisting law of trademarks. Referring to the findings in a case involving, in part, provisions of the then newly passed California dilution statute,[4] a federal court, over 25 years ago, said, "Until this statute is interpreted more fully by a California court, we feel constrained not to give it an overly broad interpretation lest it swallow up all competition in the claim of protection of trade name infringement."

So to what extent does real public policy exist concerning use of trademarks where there is no likelihood of confusion on the part of the public? There has certainly been a tendency in recent years to protect trademarks that have achieved some prominence against use by others who would trade on the marks' consumer franchise although no harm was done to consumers by the usurping users. Many academics writing in the marketing arena take a pro-trademark-owner stance, viewing firms' trademarks as assets, part of their intellectual property and evidence of an earned position in the marketplace not to be sullied by use by others.

The common marketing term for the value of a successful mark is "brand equity," and possession of such equity is ordinarily viewed favorably.[5,6] Historically, what has now become brand equity was carried on the books of many companies as "good will" and was recognized as having monetary value. However, at one point in the late 1970s the Federal Trade Commission (FTC) asked the Trademark and Patent Office to cancel the FORMICA® trademark on the grounds that it had become a generic mark and no longer benefited the public, restraining competition. The FTC's claim was that the public was likely to be misled as to the function of the word FORMICA, purchasing the allegedly now-generic brand without giving consideration to similar products of competitors because the competitors' products might appear to be other than the "real" product they sought.[7] In other words, the success of the proprietors of the FORMICA mark in creating strong brand equity for their mark was sought to be punished by depriving them of the rights to that mark! The requested action was not, however, taken, and FORMICA remains a trademark rather than a generic name. It is not so much that a petition to cancel the mark was filed, it is that the petition was filed not by a competitor but by the government agency charged with maintaining competitive conditions in the U.S. marketplace. Public policy, if indeed it exists, thus seems confused as to which actions and what sorts of trademark protection are appropriate to best serve the interests of the public at large.

5. The eight dilution criteria effectively denied protection to a large number of trademarks. New marks only recently created or only recently registered were, in general, probably not protectable under the 1995 statute. Moreover, though injunctive relief was in theory available under the law, the eight criteria for establishing the fame and distinctiveness of a mark and the necessity to test the achievement of those criteria argued against the likelihood of many summary judgments (judgments based on the content of the law rather than the arguments of the litigants) being handed down in actions involving this issue.

Since the implementation of the 1995 Act, we have been experiencing a case of gestation of public policy. The phrasing of the criteria advanced by the statute was subject to interpretation, which is one of the functions of the federal court system. As litigation proceeded under the statute, the various circuit and appellate courts produced written interpretations and decisions concerning the concepts and criteria involved in the issue of dilution. New law appearing as common law was invoked and previously unthought-of arguments brought to the courtroom.

Let us consider "blurring" in this context. "Trademark dilution by blurring occurs when the public sees a famous mark and thinks of the junior mark's products."[8] Under the 1995 law the courts interpreted blurring in a number of different ways. Some courts interpreted the term to mean that the famous mark failed to operate as a unique product source identifier.[9] Others connected the blurring concept with loss of revenues (*Ringling Bros. Barnum and Bailey Combined Shows v. Utah Div. of Travel Dev.*, 130 F. 3d 449, 457 (4th Cir., 1999); *Moseley v. V Secret Catalogue, Inc.*, 537 U.S. 418, 433 (2003)). The Seventh Circuit used a two-prong test to ascertain dilution by blurring (Eli Lilly, 233 F.3d at 466, 469) while the Second, Third, and Sixth Circuits used an analysis based on ten factors (see *Nabisco Inc. v. PF Brands Inc.*, 191 F.3d 208, 217–222 (2d Cir. 1999)).

According to the 1995 Act, "tarnishment" occurred "when the image of a famous trademark was degraded by unauthorized use of an identical or similar (copycat) variation of the famous mark on junior products of inferior quality or with unwholesome images.[10,11] The federal courts in applying the law have typically held that dilution by tarnishment occurs when the famous mark is used by nonowners in connection with products of an unwholesome nature or low-quality products—in other words, as the verbiage of the law provided.

6. Exemptions from Provisions of the 1995 Dilution Act. Some uses of trademarks by nonowners were, incidentally, specifically exempted from the provisions of the 1995 law as free speech rights. These included "fair use" of a mark in the context of comparative commercial advertising or promotion, noncommercial uses of the mark such as parody, satire, and editorial commentary, and all forms of news reporting and news commentary. One wonders at the limits to which the categories of parody and satire may be carried. Is it necessary that they breach the bounds of libel before they may be considered to be damaging? So far as this author is aware, no cases have yet been adjudicated relevant to these specific exceptions, and there are certainly venues where it has been considered good sport to lampoon practically every class of branded product for many, many years.

7. Interpretations of the 1995 Law by the Courts: General Thrust. Ever since the 1995 statute took effect, a number of interesting cases were filed that carried the dilution argument further than was imagined in 1995. As might have been expected, the first several cases under the dilution law had to do with fairly straightforward issues that could be fairly easily classed into the categories of blurring and tarnishment.

8. Internet Applications of the 1995 Law: Thus, the use of the Internet domain name "candyland.com"—which, technically speaking, is merely an address—to promote pornographic materials on the Internet brought action from Hasbro, Inc., proprietors of the children's game of the same name[12] as a case of tarnishment (pornography construed to be an unwholesome product). Hasbro prevailed in this action.

Blurring cases also devolved from the Internet, as in the case of *Intermatic, Inc. v. Toeppen*.[13] In this instance, Toeppen had registered the trademarked name of the plaintiff as a domain name (Intermatic .com) on the Internet with the apparent intent of attempting to sell it to its normal proprietor or to others. His action (and the related action of similarly registering over 240 other famous marks as domain names) was found to blur the distinctiveness of the Intermatic mark. Note again that domain names are not trademarks, merely addresses on the Internet, but they may be construed to blur the identity of the trademark owners if, when accessed, they are found to be the property of someone else—or worse, are discovered to be for sale to the highest bidder. The dilution statute has also proven useful for firms seeking to protect their interest in their right to use their own names. It should be pointed out, however, that if the intent of the registrant of a domain name were legitimate, the protection established in the Toeppen case might not apply. Thus, if one were to acquire the domain name "jeep.org" or "jeep.net" for one's historical site summarizing the history of the vehicle or as a contact name for Jeep owners or collectors, it would be doubtful that Chrysler LLC could or would claim dilution.

9. Further Expansion of the 1995 Law's Coverage by Interpretation: Additional interesting new cases created apparent expansion of the coverage of the law by court interpretation. One aspect of dilution left unclear in the original statement of the 1995 law involved the issue of "exact copying." In other words, was it necessary that the alleged infringement be the result of an exact rendering of the words or graphics of the original trademark to be dilution? Several cases set this issue to rest. In *Anheuser-Busch, Inc. v. Andy's Sportswear*,[14] the court agreed with plaintiff that use of the term "Buttwiser" on T-shirts parodying the "Budweiser" beer trademark was a diluting alteration of the original use. This, and the contemporaneous decision in a case in Pennsylvania involving litigation by the owners of the "famous" mark WAWA for a chain of over 500 convenience stores against the proprietor of a single convenience store styled HAHA[15] in which the WAWA interests were upheld, apparently overturned the previous appellate decision in *Mead Data Central, Inc. v. Toyota Motor Sales, Inc.*,[16] which found that the terms LEXIS and LEXUS were not sufficiently similar (not identically similar) and thus not subject to an interpretation of dilution. Of course, the latter case was adjudicated prior to the passage of the 1995 federal statute.

In the more recent case of *Icee Distributors, Inc. v. J & J Snack Foods Corp. and WalMart Stores, Inc.*,[17] in which the author was expert for the defendants, a federal district court in Louisiana held that the owner of a trademark (Icee) had diluted the rights of its licensee by pursuing a brand extension that applied the trademark to a line of products designed for sale to a different market segment than that in which the licensee operated. This decision seemingly flies in the face of the provision of the law that specifically extends the protection of the statute to the owners of trademarks, not their licensees.

In a case that received significant press coverage for several years (*Moseley d/b/a/ Victor's Little Secret v. Victoria's Secret Catalogue, Inc.*),[18] the Supreme Court, in March of 2003, unanimously agreed that the defendant (Victor's) had intentionally traded on the much-better-known name of the plaintiff in a fashion that constituted dilution by blurring, granting an injunction against Moseley on that premise. The Court also held, however, that no dollar damages to the plaintiff had resulted because of the obvious inferiority (a single storefront) of the defendant and the defendant's products to the plaintiff and its products. Whether this decision was related to the fact that both firms dealt in sexually enticing products, which may have tainted the court's opinion on what constitutes dilution, remains to be seen. In effect, the court seems to have agreed that the existence of dilution by blurring does not necessarily imply that a loss of sales or profits results. The impact of this decision was viewed by many to be a significant weakening of the 1995 Dilution Act's capacity to protect the owners of name brands.[19]

However, the Second Circuit Court of Appeals held[20] that Nabisco could not distribute a fish-shaped cracker similar to that of Pepperidge Farms' "Goldfish" because of the blurring that would occur, and that Pepperidge Farms (PF) did not have to provide proof of actual dilution because of the cost or difficulty of providing such proof.[21] PF's product itself was held to be both distinctive and famous and, on that basis alone, PF was granted a preliminary injunction against Nabisco.

10. Trade Dress as a Broadening of Interpretation of Dilution: A Brief Synopsis. Finally, the 1995 Trademark Dilution Act opened new

doors to the concept of "trade dress" as a market differentiator, hence as a component of one's protectable interest. Trade dress has long been defined as a unique component of the physical appearance of a product or its packaging that differentiates it from the products of others. A classic example of trade dress is the wasp-waisted bottle traditionally used in the packaging of Coca-Cola, which has long since been acknowledged to be unique to that company and part of its protectable assets. The Coca-Cola bottle is inherently distinctive, defining the product within and confirming the buyer's expectations. Other components of trade dress may be distinctive through secondary meaning—that of identifying the product's source rather than the product itself.[22]

In *Wal-Mart Stores, Inc. v. Samara Brothers, Inc.,*[23] the Supreme Court, reacting to the concept that confusion of the customer was no longer a requirement for the extension of trademark protection against all kinds of users of similar marks, stiffened the requirement for proof of distinctiveness of product design by demanding a showing of secondary meaning (i.e., that the product's design or packaging uniquely identifies its proprietor). The differentiation between product design and product packaging as trade dress creates a greater burden of proof on the part of plaintiffs seeking to protect elements of product design.

The *Nabisco v. PF* case mentioned earlier contained an element of product design trade dress in the shape of the crackers that were part of the dilution action. These were held to be distinctive by secondary meaning, being directly identifiable and well known as the PF product. The court did not, in fact, require PF to prove this secondary distinctiveness, but rather accepted it as a common sense fact based on the concept that irremediable damage would likely be done before proof of loss could be accumulated and presented to the court.

Other cases that have come to the attention of this writer relate to litigations involving the use of color in trade dress. Though the Supreme Court has held that color can never be inherently distinctive, there has been at least one recent case in which the color—and only the color—of the package of the product in question was a central issue in the litigation. The case was settled out of court and the litigants cannot be named here, but the alleged infringing product has been removed from the market.

The Trademark Dilution Revision Act of 2006

11. Genesis of the 2006 Law: Why Change the Existing Statute? Two years after the Supreme Court's decision in *Moseley d/b/a Victor's Little Secret v. Victoria's Secret Catalogue, Inc.* (supra, also as 537 U.S. 418), Congress reacted by proposing new trademark dilution legislation (H.R. 683 of the 109th Congress), which was enacted on March 8, 2006, thus becoming the Trademark Dilution Revision Act of 2006 (15 USC 1051 revising 15 USC 1125). This law completely strikes the definition of trademark dilution in the Federal Trademark Dilution Act and the language of that act regarding dilution remedies. It substitutes a new definition specifically recognizing dilution by blurring and tarnishment and defining both and provides injunctive relief to holders of famous marks whose marks have been diluted by either or both of these causes. Such relief is deemed appropriate regardless of the presence or absence of actual or likely confusion, of competition, or of actual economic injury. The law does not prohibit seeking relief in addition to injunctive relief in the event that confusion, competition, or actual economic injury shall have occurred as a result of the actions of the holder of the junior mark.

The 2006 law defines a mark to be famous if it is "widely recognized by the general consuming public of the United States as a designation of source of the goods or services of the mark's owner (120 Stat. 1730, Sec. 2, ¶ 2A)." Within the same section, the law also identifies four relevant factors that should be considered in making the determination of the fame of a mark. These are:

A. the duration, extent, and geographic reach of advertising and publicity of the mark, whether advertised or publicized by the owner or third parties;

B. the amount, volume, and geographic extent of sales of goods or services offered by the mark;

C. the extent of actual recognition of the mark; and

D. whether the mark was registered under the Act of March 3, 1881, or the Act of February 20, 1905, or on the principal register.

The above enumeration is certainly more specific than the eight factors suggested in the 1995 law but is not all inclusive, the new law stating that the court may and should consider ALL relevant factors of which it is aware but specifying only those stated above.

In discussing whether a mark or trade name is likely to cause dilution by blurring, the revised law takes a similar approach, stating (120 Stat. 1731, Sec. 2B) that ALL relevant factors should be considered but naming only the following:

A. the degree of similarity between the mark or trademark and the famous mark;

B. the degree of inherent or acquired distinctiveness of the famous mark;

C. the extent to which the owner of the famous mark is engaging in substantially exclusive use of the mark;

D. the degree of recognition of the famous mark;

E. whether the user of the mark or trade name intended to create an association with the famous mark; and

F. any actual association between the mark or the trade name and the famous mark.

Dilution by tarnishment is defined in the revised law as "association arising from the similarity between a mark or trade name and a famous mark that harms the reputation of the famous mark (120 STAT 1731, Sec. 2C)." No mention is made of the inferior or unwholesome qualities of the junior mark, the sole requirement being its capacity to harm the reputation of the famous mark.

12. The 2006 statute also preserves the concept of "fair use," excluding from actions for dilution by blurring or tarnishment "any fair use," including nominative or descriptive fair use, or facilitation of fair use, of a famous mark by another person other than as a designation of source for the person's own goods or services, including use in connection with

A. advertising or promotion that permits consumers to compare goods or services; or

B. identifying and parodying, criticizing, or commenting upon the famous mark owner or the goods or services of the famous mark owner.

The statute also preserves the right to use famous marks as part of any news reporting and news commentary and also in any form of noncommercial use of a mark (120 Stat. 1731 Sec. 3A).

The 2006 Act also places a heavier burden of proof in civil actions for trade dress dilution by stating that the person asserting such trade dress protection must now prove that

A. the trade dress protection claimed, taken as a whole, is not functional and is famous; and

B. if the claimed trade dress includes any mark or marks registered on the principal register, the unregistered matter, taken as a whole, is famous separate and apart from any fame of such registered marks (120 Stat. 1731 Sec. 4).

Other language in the act makes persons who use a mark or trade name that is likely to cause dilution by blurring or tarnishment after the date of the enactment of the act liable or injunction if they willfully intended to trade on the recognition of the famous mark or by reason of dilution by tarnishment, they willfully intended to harm the reputation of the famous mark (120 Stat. 1732 Sec. 6).

The 2006 Act also bars the holders of trademarks registered under the Trademark Act of March 3, 1881, or that of February 20, 1965, or in the principal register under the 2006 Act from action against them that claims that they have blurred or tarnished their own trademark or that seeks damages caused by harm to the distinctiveness of their mark or reputation of their mark by the markholder (see *ICEE Distributors v. J & J Snack Foods, Inc.* (supra))

Thus, on the whole, the desired effect of the Trademark Dilution Revision Act was to clarify the definitions of what trademark dilution was, how it might occur, and to indicate how and when trademark holders might consider litigation to protect their rights, and similarly, what rights others might have, such as the right to fair use over trademarks not owned by them. At the first instance, at least, some of these objectives seem to have been met.

13. Some Additional Comments on Trademark Dilution. No one ever said that the legal arena was simple or that the written language of the law is necessarily consistent with the interpretation to which it will be subjected by the courts. The now not-so-new Trademark Dilution Act of 1995 seems to have had a rather significant effect on the quantum of protection provided to trademarks and their related intellectual property rights. The 2006 Trademark Dilution Revision Act was aimed at clarifying terms and definitions left unclear in the prior legislation. Whether the newer law will ultimately prove to be the desired panacea remains to be seen. However, in this context perhaps it is better to note that the thrust of protection for intellectual property rights as embodied in the trademark statutes has, over the past decade, been significantly broadened and included in that broadening is protection to cover what one might call "noncompetitive" use of the same trademarks. If one adds to this the recent legal interpretations of the concept of "trade dress" and the apparent extension of much broader coverage to that aspect of product composition, it would appear that the effect of the legislative and judicial components of the protection of property rights has been to significantly broaden those rights, perhaps at the expense of some muddying of the waters concerning the nature, extent, and implications of that broadening.

Summary

Trademarks are eligible for three levels of legal protection under U.S. law. The weakest level of protection is common law, the next being protection offered under state law, and the last and strongest is that offered by registration in the Principal Register of Marks at the federal level. The ordinary sequence of actions in the event that direct infringement (involving direct copying of the trademark) is apparent is negotiation with the alleged infringer; failing that, suit in an appropriate court of jurisdiction is the next course. If indirect infringement appears to be the case, recourse to the provisions of the Trademark Dilution Revision Act of 2006 may be appropriate. This law provides protection for trademark owners whose famous marks have lost value because of the actions of persons with other marks that caused "blurring" of the identity of the famous mark due to the similarity of their mark or its method of use or by "tarnishment" where their mark harmed the reputation of the famous mark. Though the terms are not used in the law, there has historically been an interpretation of "tarnishment" that associated the offending mark with "unsavory" or "inferior" qualities with respect to the famous mark.

CHAPTER 7

Trade Dress

More on This Newly Expanding Class of Trademarks

And the First Shall be Last and the Last First?
Trade Dress in a Historical Context

An Older Form of Communication Is Revived. The concept of trade dress is not new in the generic sense: that is, as a means of identifying the product of a vendor or the vendor himself or herself by visual cues. In Imperial Roman times, when literacy was the exception rather than the rule, many tradespeople identified themselves by the use of symbols attached to their places of business or by a distinctive mode of dress adopted by members of the trade. Thus, only senators wore purple and the military red. Some of the symbols developed during this period were the surgeon–barber's red and white striped pole, the three gold balls of the moneylender (pawnbroker), the model sailing ship of the merchant trader (as in the Hanseatic League), the dried bush before the door of the brewer, and the suspended wine barrel of the spirits merchant. Numbers of these symbols remain in use to this day and may be familiar to the reader.

Over time, trade symbols became vendor specific. It became the custom, beginning nearly 700 years ago, for British alehouses to bear names using visual symbols as identifiers. A number of these, still in use, include the White Swan, the Rose and Crown, the Cock and Bull, the Dog and Bear, the Royal Oak, and the Wheel and Anchor. In each case, the pub owner[1] used his choice of name and identifying symbol to "stake a claim" to the drinking trade in the area (usually of less than a mile radius or so) surrounding his place, and fellow tapmen were expected to respect the original name-holder's choice within that area. To fail in this expectation could bring physical retribution. Proprietors located a noncompeting distance away could use the same identifier claimed by another pub operator. The primary function of the choice of name was so that persons seeking a pub could be directed to one nearby by describing its symbol, which they could understand despite the inability to read.

Of interest for the purposes of this chapter is the very recent realization by many marketers of the importance of trade dress to product identification and differentiation where reading, in the conventional sense, is difficult either because of individual monolinguality in multilingual markets on the one hand and the pace of modern life where reading highway billboards and similar presentations of information, even if one normally reads the language well, is not only difficult but also dangerous. Both conditions have highlighted the need for understanding the importance of trade dress. Later, we will examine recent legal cases that have broken new ground in the interpretation and creation of new examples of modern trade dress.

Domestic Bases for Trade Dress Protection: The Situation in the United States

1. In the United States, trade dress may be protected as intellectual property in the same way as any other trademark. Under the Lanham Act, last amended in 2006, any "word, name, symbol, or device, or any combination thereof" that is used "to identify and distinguish goods or services, including a unique product, from those manufactured or sold by others (15 USC 1127)" can be registered as a trademark in either the principal or the supplemental register. Successful registration of trade dress constitutes prima facie evidence that use of the same dress by others within the United States is an infringement.

   Unlike in civil law countries, where registration of trademarks is usually mandatory to protect the marks from infringement, registration is not mandatory in the United States to provide protection. Should a trade dress proprietor desire not to register his or her trade dress under the Lanham Act but it nonetheless falls under the definition stated in the slightly more expansive phrase "word, name, term, symbol, or device, or any combination thereof" … used in trade …

"on or in connection with any goods or services, or any container for goods" found in (15 USC 1125(a)) it is protected on a common law basis. Demonstrating first and continuous use of the trade dress in comparison with the use history of an alleged infringer is sufficient to claim domestic protection.

2. Assuring Domestic Protection of Unregistered Trade Dress: The Standards

The following standards have been set by the findings of the various U.S. courts that have been called upon to rule in cases germane to the ownership and protection of intellectual property under common law and thus are subject to change on the basis of judicial interpretation of facts and applicable law and legislative review and revision.

A. Distinctiveness of the Dress

Unregistered trade dress is automatically entitled to legal protection in the United States without a show of proof if it is "inherently distinctive." The Coca-Cola bottle is inherently distinctive because of its unique shape. If the trade dress is descriptive in some way of product function or use, it is entitled to legal protection upon a show of proof that it has "acquired" distinctiveness (secondary meaning). The usual test of secondary meaning is if consumers, or members of the appropriate market segment if the product is not a consumer good, immediately identify the trade dress with the product in or on which it appears. If, however, the trade dress is generic—neither inherently distinctive nor possessing secondary meaning, it receives no protection. Determination of inherent distinctiveness is a matter for the courts and the tests used vary from jurisdiction to jurisdiction and with the nature of the product.

B. Nonfunctionality of the Dress

In addition to being distinctive, unregistered trade dress cannot be functional if it is to be entitled to protection. A claim that a product feature is nonfunctional may be part of a plaintiff's (trademark owner's) prima facie case against an alleged infringer or the counterclaim that it *is* functional may be raised by a defendant as an affirmative defense. To be functional, the trade dress must be "essential to the use or purpose of the article or affect the cost or quality of the article."[2] The term "essential" means the presence of a trade dress feature must be dictated by the function it is to perform.[3] To be nonfunctional, a product's alleged trade dress must *fail* to possess the stated characteristics.

C. Likelihood of Confusion Between Two Versions of Dress

Distinctiveness (whether inherent or acquired) and nonfunctionality are not ordinarily sufficient to establish the validity of a claim of violation of protected trade dress. In addition, the plaintiff claiming infringement must ordinarily establish that the appropriated features of the protected trade dress, as used by the alleged infringer, result in two (or more) products that are confusingly similar.[4] The same tests are used for trade dress as bases for judgment by the courts against alleged infringers as are used for other trademark infringements: (a) the strength of the plaintiff's trade dress; (b) relatedness of the goods; (c) similarity of the trade dresses; (d) evidence of actual confusion on the part of would-be purchasers; (e) the marketing channels used; (f) likely degree of purchaser care; (g) defendant's intent in selecting the trade dress used; and (h) likelihood of expansion of defendant's market share as a result of choice of the trade dress used.

3. A New Caution: Potential for the Alleged Infringement to Dilute the Value of the Dress

Implementation of the U.S. Trademark Dilution Act of 1995 and its subsequent amendment by the Trademark Dilution Revision Act of 2006 have recognized that, under certain conditions, it is not necessary for actual consumer confusion to be caused by the actions of an infringer for damages to be awarded if the results of the infringer's actions cause a loss of value of the trademark to its owner by either "blurring" or "tarnishment."

Blurring occurs when the presence of the infringing dress reflects negatively on the senior trade dress simply by its presence so that the senior loses value. Proving blurring is a difficult process because blurring is the result, not the intent, of the action in question. Thus, a claim of tarnishment is somewhat easier to prove because its basis is that the action of the alleged infringer places the protected dress in a position of being associated with unsavory or unflattering actions or events.

In the event that none of the conditions outlined, that is, distinctiveness, nonfunctionality, and likelihood of confusion, are present with respect to the plaintiff's product characteristics and their appropriation by the alleged infringer, the claim of the plaintiff against the alleged infringer becomes moot. On occasion, it is possible that the presence of appropriation of only two of the characteristics, distinctiveness and nonfunctionality, may suffice to uphold the claim if their result is to create a loss of value of the plaintiff's property due to blurring or tarnishment.

However, it is also likely that a substantial number of claims of infringement are upheld despite lack of the intent to infringe on the part of the alleged infringer because actions they may have taken in good faith create a product that meets the three criteria for infringement.

Registering Trade Dress: It's the Same as for Any Other Trademark

The standards for registration of trade dress in the United States are the same as those for traditional written or graphic marks (15 USC 1052, 1091). In practice, however, the Patent and Trademark Office (PTO) systematically rejects trade dress applications on the basis that the claimed feature or features is (are) descriptive; rejections on the basis of functionality are also common. The process of overcoming these rejections by proving secondary meaning or nonfunctionality can be expensive and must be weighed against the value of registration.[5]

On the Tendency to Fail to Register Trade Dress As a Protectable Property Right

Since the definition of trade dress includes all and any of the various features enumerated as possible components, the process of claiming trade dress as property must consider the totality of the features that the owner believes distinguish his or her product from its competitors under the definition. In the decision in *Smith, Kline, and French Co. v. Premo Pharmaceutical*

Laboratories,[6] the court stated that "Trade dress is a complex composite of features and the law of unfair competition in respect to trade dress requires that all of the features be considered together, not separately." The same language was quoted in *American Greetings Corporation v. Dan-Dee Imports, Incorporated* and further affirmed for the same parities in 625 F. 2d 1055 (3d Cir. 1980). Other cases reinforced these statements: *John J. Harland Co. v. Clarke Checks, Inc.*, in which the court specifically mentioned "size, shape, color or color combinations, texture, graphics, and even sales techniques" for bank checks and *Blue Bell Bio-Medical v. Cin-Bad, Inc,* in which trade dress was identified as a business' "total image and overall appearance."

The above interpretations of trade dress mandate that a claimant seeking registration enumerates all of the features that contribute to the whole of the claimed trade dress, even though some of them have been used previously by others. In effect, the U.S. courts have held that one cannot be denied protection for one's trade dress because it is composed of components such as letters of the alphabet or colors from the common palette simply because they have been used before. Thus, a claim that a bottle is trade dress because it possesses a unique shape or is tinted a particular color (or both) cannot be denied because it is a bottle or is round or is green—or any of the above features. In fact, ALL of those features probably comprise part of that which should be claimed unless, taken together, they are seen to be too similar to someone else's bottle used for the same or a similar purpose to be distinctive. In this vein, John Deere Company's claim of trade dress protection for its green paint is neither positively nor negatively affected by the fact that the products of the company are painted or that paint protects from rust. This is a practice dictated by product function involving the product's exposure to weather. The trade dress aspect of the paint is that it is a particular shade of green, just as Caterpillar tractors are yellow and International Harvester red.

The presence of generic or descriptive elements in trade dress also does not necessarily render the trade dress unprotectable. The test often relies on an analysis of industry practice. It is difficult, for example, to design an inherently distinctive beer bottle because the packaging practices of the brewing industry require that such bottles be filled, capped, and labeled on standard machines and fit standard racks on delivery trucks and in stores and, thus, within certain fairly narrow allowable limits, must be of a certain height, not exceed a certain circumference, usually (in the United States) contain 12 ounces (355 milliliters), and, in the interest of beer freshness, be either brown or green in color. To create a unique trade dress under these constraints argues for an approach recognizing that the absence of one or more of these features, rather than their presence, might be a basis for trade dress. A clear bottle, or one shorter and fatter than the norm, or even one whose label "goes against the grain" of typical beer bottle labeling by being nontraditional in design but otherwise meets all of the specifications for protected trade dress listed above might be sufficiently different to qualify as trade dress even though it remains a beer bottle and that function is not disguised by the trade dress feature. Thus the Haig and Haig "Pinch" Scotch whiskey bottle and the Coca-Cola original bottle, recently reintroduced in a 2-liter size, are both protected as registered trademarks in the principal register. See *Ex Parte Haig and Haig, Ltd.,* 118 USPQ 229 (1958) and, for Coca-Cola, Register Nos. 696,147 and 1,057,884.

In the process of protecting one's trade dress by registration, one should recognize that, in the event that litigation should become necessary, a would-be infringer is likely to make a defense based on picking the features of the plaintiff's trade dress apart and attacking each of them individually. Such actions have been recognized as inappropriate for a very long time, and an attack against them based on forcing an examination of the trade dress claim "en bloc" by the court is entirely appropriate and often successful. See *O. and W. Thum Company v. Dickenson,* 245 F. 609 (6th Cir. 1917), *certiorari denied,* 246 US 664 (1918). This now 90-year-old decision laid the foundation for "trade dress as a whole" judicial examination of such issues.

Trade dress originating in a foreign country to which trademark protection has been extended by that country is automatically extended protection in the United States and other countries signatory to the Paris Convention, provided the original country extending protection to the trade dress is a signatory of the Paris Convention. The conditions under which such protection was extended by the foreign jurisdiction, whether they be "common law" or "statutory," are irrelevant, so long as the law of the protecting country defines them as adequate. Similar conditions apply when U.S. trademarks are used by their holders in other nations signatory to the Convention.

Recent Judicial Expansions of Trade Dress Protection by U.S. Courts

As has been seen, the definition of trade dress is quite broad. In recent years, use of this definition has resulted in the extension of trade dress protection to an assortment of assets that would, in an earlier period, have been considered outside the scope of the law. Among these have been the ambiance (or atmosphere) of restaurants, the design of golf holes, the shape and appearance of a number of products, use of specific colors (as property), and even more exotic items.

A. Ambiance

    i. *Architecture and Interior Design*

      In what many view as having been one of the most significant U.S. trade dress cases to date, *Two Pesos, Incorporated v. Taco Cabana, Incorporated*,[7] the Supreme Court of the United States, in a rare example of that court hearing a trademark case, held that the trade dress of Taco Cabana's Restaurants was protected, and described it as "a festive eating atmosphere having interior dining and patio areas decorated with artifacts, bright colors, paintings, and murals. The patio includes interior and exterior areas with the interior patio capable of being sealed off from the outside patio by overhead garage doors. The stepped exterior of the building is a festive and vivid color scheme using top border paint and neon stripes. Bright awnings and umbrellas continue the theme."

      The infringing trade dress was identified by the court only as "very similar" to Taco Cabana's. This case represents the first time that "ambiance" or "atmosphere" was found to be a protectable instance of trade dress.

      In the case of *Fuddruckers, Incorporated v. Doc's B. R. Others, Incorporated*,[8] the U.S. Ninth Circuit Court of Appeals held that Fuddrucker's "décor, menu, layout, and style" was protectable trade dress. The court specifically noted that protectable components of the above features were food preparation areas visible to customers, bulk food items stored in the dining area, and certain aspects of the tile, mirrors, style of seating, and even the presence of a bakery area in the restaurant. This earlier decision by the lower court reinforces the scope of the Supreme Court's ultimate finding.

ii. *Copycat Golf Holes*

Certain golf courses are known for their "signature" holes, holes that are in some way unique and distinctive. Since no two golf courses are exactly alike, the fame of some of these holes—because of their very uniqueness—has been established for a long time. In 1996, the degree to which copycat golf holes constituted infringement of other golf courses, holes was litigated (*Pebble Beach Company v. Tour 18 I, Limited*).[9] It was alleged that Tour 18 operated two public golf courses at which copies of holes from famous courses elsewhere in the country were featured. Plaintiffs alleged infringement of the service marks as well as the trade dress represented by the individual holes that had been replicated at the defendant's courses.

At issue in this case were holes at Pebble Beach golf course, Pinehurst golf course number 2, and the course at Harbour Town (at Sea Pines). The court specifically examined Pebble Beach hole number 14, Pinehurst hole number 2, and Harbour Town hole 18, the so-called Lighthouse Hole, for inherent distinctiveness. Trade dress protection for the first two holes was denied, because, while the courses at which they were located were, indeed, famous, the holes copied by Tour 18 were not the "signature" holes at those courses, and were not sufficiently "arbitrary and distinctive as compared to other golf holes such that the design automatically serve[d] as identifiers of source." Harbour Town hole number 18, however, because it included an actual lighthouse, a truly unusual design feature for a golf hole, was found to have appropriate characteristics for inherent distinctiveness of design. Ultimately, based on this determination, the court concluded that there was likelihood of confusion between Tour 18's courses and Harbour Town's, and ordered Tour 18 to remove its replicas of the Harbour Town lighthouse from their golf courses. They were not required to change the architecture or actual playing surfaces of the relevant holes themselves.

B. Alternative Sensory Stimuli as Trade Dress

  i. *Sounds as Trade Dress*

   It is possible to protect a sound as trade dress in the United States, providing the sound meets the purpose of identifying a specific source of goods or services and can be otherwise then self-described. Among the sounds that have been registered in the United States are Tarzan's yell (USPTO No.2210506, Serial No. 75326989, Edgar Rice Burroughs, Inc.), Alfred Newman's famous orchestral fanfare (usually played under the visual presentation of a stylized tower with spotlights) (USPTO No. 2000732, Serial No. 74629287, Twentieth Century Fox Film Corporation), and the roar of Leo the Lion (USPTO No. 139550, Serial No. 73553567, Metro-Goldwin-Mayer Film Corporation).

   Several years ago (in 1994), Harley-Davidson Company, the Minnesota maker of motorcycles, sought to register as trade dress the sound of their V-twin motorcycle engine, claiming it was unique and otherwise met all the requirements for registration under the World Trade Organization's broadened criteria (see *World Trade Organization Agreement on Trade-Related Aspects of Intellectual Property Rights, Section 15-1*, which broadened the legal definition of trademark to encompass "any sign ... capable of distinguishing the goods or services of one undertaking from those of other undertakings"). Nine of Harley's competitors filed motions in opposition to the Harley's application, noting that Harley's version of this engine had been in production since 1909 and that they had all been making similar engines for a significant number of years. Harley quietly abandoned their application for registration in the year 2000.

  ii. *The Use of Colors*

   In *Qualitex Co. v. Jacobson Products*,[10] the U.S. Supreme Court settled a disagreement among the various Circuit Courts by ruling that a specific color can be protected and registered as a trademark. *Qualitex* had claimed a green-gold color as a trademark of their dry-cleaning pads, bringing action against competitor Jacobson who had begun to sell a similarly colored pad for the same use. Owens-Corning Company has obtained a number of registrations for the color pink as used on its Fiberglas® insulation products. The use of this color serves no known functional purpose. Moreover, its use increases the cost of production of the products, but definitely identifies the source of the proprietor's wares.

For other findings in this area of color protection, see *Par Pharmaceuticals, Inc. v. Searle Pharmaceuticals, Inc.*,[11] and *Merck Co. v. Par Pharmaceuticals, Inc.*,[12] 770 F. 2d 1072 (3d Cir.), cert. denied, 474 US 981 (1985) (blue and white capsule color protected).

C. Shape and Appearance

i. *Unregistered Marks*

"Form (ever) follows function," said the nineteenth-century American architect Louis Sullivan, and to a substantial extent this is true. However, when it is possible to design a product in a number of different ways, at least some of which possess nonfunctional features, the possibility of the creation of trade dress exists. In this connection, the so-called *Abercrombie* categories became important. In *Abercrombie and Fitch Co. v. Hunting World, Inc.*,[13] Judge Henry J. Friendly, a respected juror noted for his incisive opinions, classified marks "in categories of generally increasing distinctiveness." The categories were (a) generic, (b) descriptive, (c) suggestive, (d) arbitrary, and (e) fanciful. Of these five categories, the last three, because it was considered to be their intrinsic nature to identify the particular source of a product, were deemed inherently distinctive and thereby entitled to protection. The various federal courts for several years referred to the *Abercrombie* categories in one way or another in their handling of cases dealing with product shape and appearance.

The Third Circuit rejected the *Abercrombie* categories outright, and instead created its own approach, seeking to decide whether a product's shape and appearance was inherently distinctive by asking whether it was "unusual and memorable, serving primarily as a designator of the source of the product." See *Krueger International Inc. v. Nightingale Inc.*[14] The basis for this point of view was twofold. First, the categories were held not to translate well to the context of shape and appearance; and second, the Supreme

Court's endorsement of the categories in *Two Pesos* applied, in this court's opinion, more to packaging than to shape and appearance, and was thus not controlling.

The Eighth Circuit, however, elected to apply the *Abercrombie* configurations in shape and appearance cases, automatically extending protection to products they felt to be in the latter three categories and only on showing secondary meaning to products in the descriptive category. According to this court, the Supreme Court's *Two Pesos* decision did not allow distinctions among trade dress types that permitted of differing tests. See *Stuart Hall Co., Inc. v. Ampad Corp.*[15]

The Second Circuit, acknowledging that the *Abercrombie* categories did not work well in shape and appearance cases, elected not to come down specifically on either the Eighth or the Third Circuit's side of the issue, instead only asking whether the product's shape and appearance were likely to "serve primarily as a designator of origin." *See Laureyssens v. Idea Group, Inc.*, 964 F. 2d. 131 (2d Cir. 1992);[16] *Knitwaves, Inc. v. Lollytogs Ltd.*, 71 F. 3d 996 (2d Cir. 1995).[17]

The Fifth Circuit refused to take any position on the issue. See *Sunbeam Products, Inc. v. The West Bend Co.*[18]

In 1996, Samara Brothers, Inc. brought suit against Wal-Mart, a number of other retailers, and manufacturer Judy-Philippine, claiming that Wal-Mart's and the others' sale of Judy-Philippine-made "knock-offs" of a line of children's clothes produced by Samara was in violation of copyrights duly granted to Samara on the design of those clothes and, among other things, for violation of 15 USC 1125(a), infringement of unregistered trade dress. All defendants except Wal-Mart settled before trial. A jury found for Samara on all counts. Wal-Mart renewed a motion for judgment as a matter of law, claiming that there was insufficient evidence to support a conclusion that Samara's clothing was protectable as distinctive trade dress under the above-stated part of the Code (which also constituted section 43(a) of the Lanham Act). The District Court denied the motion and awarded Samara $1.6 million in damages and also injunctive relief. The denial was affirmed by the Second Circuit Court of Appeals (165 F. 3d 120 (1998)). The case was carried to the Supreme Court of the United States on writ of certiorari (165 F. 3d, reversed and remanded; 529 US 205 (2000)). The Court, in an opinion written by Justice Scalia, found that design was *never* inherently distinctive because it "almost invariably serves purposes other than source identification," and therefore that "a product's design is distinctive, and therefore protectable, ONLY upon a showing of secondary meaning." This landmark decision thus made it significantly more difficult for proprietors to protect the shape and appearance of their products from copying than had previously been the case.

ii. *Registered Marks*

A number of product shapes and appearances have succeeded in obtaining trademark registration. Some examples of registered marks and case findings that have arisen out of these registrations are:

(a) Tizio Brand halogen desk lamps

When defendant sought to copy the design of this desk lamp, which is included in the permanent design collection of the Museum of Modern Art, a preliminary injunction was granted to estop. *See Artemide Sp.A. v. Grandlite Design and Manufacturing Co., Ltd.*[19]

(b) The Ferrari "Daytona" Spyder, Testarossa, and 365 GTB/4

Though the Court in this case used language indicating that a show of secondary meaning was necessary despite the then-new *Two Pesos* precedent, it nonetheless found that the appearance of the first two Ferrari models was protected from copying by a maker of car kits because the designs in question were "instantly identifiable" as of Ferrari origin. *See Ferrari Esercizio v. Roberts.*[20] In a separate instance, the design of the Ferrari GTB/4 was protected against replication as a toy car on the same premise in *Ferrari SpA v. McBurnie.*[21]

(c) Callaway "Big Bertha" golf clubs

Callaway Golf Company, plaintiff, obtained a preliminary injunction against sale of defendant's "Big Bursa" and "Big Brother" clubs based on the inherent distinctiveness and nonfunctionality of the trade dress of the Big Bertha clubs made and sold by Callaway, even though they also possess nondistinctive and functional elements. The court enjoined defendant using the "en bloc" definition of distinctiveness and nonfunctionality as the basis for injunction. *See Callaway Golf Company v. Golf Clean, Inc.*[22]

When competitor West Bend sought to copy the appearance of the traditional Sunbeam product, the court avoided the conflict mentioned in (c) above concerning the presence of both functional and nonfunctional features in a design, finding instead that the Sunbeam design was protected because it had acquired secondary meaning. *See Sunbeam Products, Inc. v. West Bend Co.*[23]

D. Trade Dress for Other Product Classes—Trade shows, Personal Distinctions, Structures, and Smells have achieved protection as trade dress in recent years. The following are examples of other instances in which such trade dress has been held to be protectable. In none of the cases cited were the trade dresses registered.

i. Trade shows

Trade shows may achieve protection provided their "name, date, locations, and the registration process" by which one obtains admission are found to have achieved secondary meaning. In *Toy Manufacturers v. Helmsley-Spear*,[24] the plaintiff alleged that the defendant's competing trade show was misleading to the public as to who was the sponsor of defendant's show. The defendant was enjoined from conducting the subject trade show on finding that the plaintiff's allegation was valid for the above reasons.

ii. Personal Distinctions

Two seminal cases in the personal distinctions category involve Jeff Foxworthy, a mechanical engineer turned country comedian, and another famous personality. In *Foxworthy v. Custom Tees, Inc.*, the court found that the phrase "you might be a redneck" was Foxworthy's "signature" line and thus was inherently distinctive.[25] Injunction against Custom Tees was granted on this basis.

The second case of relevance in this context involves Johnny Carson, former host of the NBC *Tonight Show*. In *Carson v. Here's Johnny Portable Toilets, Inc.* referenced by the court in the Foxworthy decision, the court found the phrase "Here's Johnny" to be identified with Johnny Carson, and thus protectable.[26] The defendant was enjoined from using that phrase in connection with the portable toilet business.

iii. Structures

Where buildings are part of a firm's identifying characteristics, they have, on occasion, received trade dress protection.[27] Among the most recent of these fairly rare occurrences was *Fotomat Corp. v. Houck* protecting the appearance of the mini-building used as a business location by Fotomat.

iv. Smells (Fragrances)

Though cases in this vein are rare, smells, like sounds, have been determined to be protectable trade dress in certain circumstances. See *In re Clarke*, in which the Trademark Trial and Appeal Board reversed the examining attorney's final rejection of application for protection and allowed registration of the "fresh, floral fragrance of plumeria blossoms" as applied to sewing thread and yarn.[28]

E. Alternative Forms of Protection for Trade Dress

Under certain circumstances, trade dress protection may be available for products, packaging, and alternatively business forms and stationery that qualify for design patents, utility patents, or copyrights.

i. Design Patents

There is no inherent conflict between protecting a product with a design patent (if such is available in the nation of primary jurisdiction) and claim of trade dress. Of particular significance in this regard is the fact that trade dress rights can provide protection for a design after the design patent has run out. The reason for this is that the source of protection in the two instances is different.

In *Krueger International Inc. v. Nightingale Inc.*, 915 F. Supp. 595 (1996), the court's opinion included the following language: "Federal trademark laws, independent in origin from design patent law, have the dual purpose of protecting both the trademark owner and the public from confusion, mistake, and deception." The case concerned the appearance of a stackable plastic chair and claim of trade dress for its design.

Having obtained a design patent may affect trade rights either positively or negatively. If the product, during the patent monopoly, becomes generic with respect to the product class because of market success, functionality of the design may be inferred and trade dress protection denied. Design patents, however, are unique to nonfunctional designs (35 USC 171). If a design patent has been granted, there is evidence that the product is nonfunctional for trade dress purposes.

ii. Utility patents

Using the law of trade dress to claim protection for a product that has been granted a utility patent, which has subsequently expired (or is unpatented), suffers from the general interpretation at law that such products are free to copy. See *Vornado Air Circulation Systems v. Duracraft Corp.* and other cases.[29]

The Vornado case added a new requirement for claiming trade dress protection for prior-patented products as follows: "where a disputed product configuration is part of a claim in a utility patent, and the configuration is a described, significant inventive aspect of the invention under 35 USC 112, so that without it the invention could not fairly be said to be the same invention, patent laws prevent its protection as trade dress, EVEN IF THE CONFIGURATION IS NONFUNCTIONAL." The last six words are a significant change from previous interpretations, which allowed for trade dress protection for nonfunctional aspects of the configuration of patented inventive products.

iii. Copyrights

Trade dress rights can be used to protect written materials such as sales brochures, form letters, and reports used in connection with promotional activities. In *Computer Care v. Service Systems Enterprises*, 982 F 2d. 1063 (7th Cir. 1992), defendant Service Systems was enjoined from using brochures, letters, and forms that were "confusingly similar" to those of the plaintiff.

The interpretation of copyrights has been extended to include even the overall appearance of a greeting card line. In *Roulo v. Russ Berrie & Co., Inc.* (886 F. 2d. 931 (7th Cir. 1989), cert. denied., 493 US 1075 (1990)), both copyright and trade dress rights were litigated, with finding for the plaintiff on basis that a line of greeting cards of her design had been "pirated" by Berrie.

Thoughts on the Future of Trade Dress

The U.S. courts, since the turn of the new century, seem to be turning away from the liberal treatment formerly given to claimants seeking to obtain trade dress protection for new trade dress forms. The trend appears to be centered on the areas of product shape and appearance and patent versus trade dress applicability.

Despite this, trade dress protection remains a valuable asset in the field of intellectual property rights. The ultimate objective of the courts remains to protect intellectual property owners, consumers, and other purchasers of goods and services from unfair market activities.

Trade dress may ultimately function as a form of intellectual property rights protection of some merit in those jurisdictions because trade dress, even when it might be ineligible for patent, copyright, or traditional trademark protection, may be actionable as a matter of principle, or on a common law, other statutory, or simply an ethical basis.

Thus, entrepreneurs should be aware of the existence of this class of intellectual property right and recognize that it does have value where other alternatives are not available or have failed.

Summary

Trade dress is a type of trademark that serves as a means of identifying the product of a vendor or the vendor him- or herself usually by means of visual, nonverbal cues. Trade dress may qualify as a trademark in the United States if the dress (e.g., the package in which the product is sold) is "inherently distinctive" because of its unusual shape. In additional to distinctiveness, nonfunctionality is also necessary if the dress is to be registered as a trademark. If for some reason the dress is NOT inherently distinctive, it may qualify for registration and thus for legal protection if it "acquires" distinctiveness, which usually means that members of the market segment to which it is directed immediately identify the trade dress with the product in or on which it appears. Confusion between the original trade dress and a similar but junior dress may cause rejection of the junior dress as a trademark. Trade dress as a trademark may be subject to dilution by "blurring" or "tarnishment" in much the same way as other trademarks. The standards for registering trade dress in the United States are the same as those for registering other trademarks, as long as the special criteria of distinctiveness, nonfunctionality, and likelihood of confusion between two similar trade dresses are satisfied. Recent decisions in the U.S. courts have allowed for a number of new types of trade dress to qualify as trademarks. Among these are the "ambiance" of restaurant architecture and interior design, the design of certain golf holes, certain sounds such as Tarzan's yell (in motion pictures), and the use of colors in building materials (pink on insulation materials from Owens-Corning). Alternative forms of protection for trade dress can be found in patent and copyright law. Under certain conditions, design patents, utility patents, and even copyrights may offer some protection for trade dress.

PART III
Defending Trade Secrets

CHAPTER 8

Keeping Secrets

Trade Secrets and Employment Contracts

When Is a Secret a Secret?

Much earlier in this text, it was stated that secrets require that they be known only to a very few people, perhaps not even in total to any single person, to remain a secret. Successfully kept trade secrets seem to be, for the most part, formulas for the mixing of ingredients resulting in a specific product or processes by which ingredients are treated using heat or pressure or some other physical manipulation to produce the desired product, or a combination of formula and process. Also earlier on in this text, the trade secrecy involving the formula for Coca-Cola concentrate and its recent transfer from a vault at SunTrust Bank in Atlanta, home of the Coca-Cola Company, in which it had resided for over 80 years, to the Company's new exhibit hall and tourist attraction, "The World of Coca-Cola," also in Atlanta, was discussed. The secret process by which Cracker Jacks are made was also commented on in the same vignette. The two secrets are different in that one involves a formula for the mixing of ingredients while in the other the ingredients are known but the process by which they are converted into the final product (the Cracker Jacks) is concealed.

There are a great many more trade secrets involving formulas and processes than the two previously discussed. The author is aware of the existence of (but does not know the details of) a number of recipes for commercially produced food products that have been matters at issue in various litigations. As an example, the mixture of beans and the roast duration and temperature involved in producing your favorite brand and style of ground coffee is probably a closely held recipe and process of its manufacturer. In those places (such as the Gulf South of the United States) where coffee mixed with chicory is popular, those mixtures and processes are guarded secrets. The same is true for brewers' formulas and processes for the production of beers.

The recipe for that great coffee cake that you so enjoy made by a local baker is quite likely known only to one person in the bakery where it is made, or in a few cases, only by a few trusted family members of the family whose bakery produces the product.

Obviously, in all of these cases someone must know what is to be mixed and in what proportions or what processes are applied to the ingredients to result in the desired changes. Thus, security of storage of the documentation of the formulas and processes involved and of the trustworthiness of the persons who must know them are the only basis on which trade secrets can be kept. The presence of nondisclosure agreements does, of course, provide protection to the extent of stating what the employee is not to reveal in terms of what they know and what the employer will seek in the event that disclosure occurs, but dollar amounts may not truly represent the damage done.

What Happens When a Secret Gets Out?

If a trade secret is somehow revealed, what remedies can be sought by the offended proprietor of the purloined thing? The issue of determining who has revealed the secret, how they gained access to it, and what their objectives were and are must first be settled. If the thief, for want of a better word, is an outsider, then he or she must be identified, found, and charged with an appropriate criminal offense or offenses, such as breaking and entering, burglary, theft, and so forth. If the matter goes to trial and they are found guilty, restitution of the value of the stolen property, fines, and a prison sentence are the likely penalties.

If the individual who has revealed the secret is an employee, the above charges may be appropriate, but so might embezzlement or fraud (for theft or illicit acquisition of assets of the firm), or violation of employment terms.

What Is a Secret Worth?

In either case, a major issue that will be raised will be the value of the stolen, purloined, or simply revealed secret. When a secret becomes no longer a secret, the value attached to the thing that was held secret diminishes. If one can make a copy of Coca-Cola that is indistinguishable from "the real thing," what remains of the "differential advantage" of the product? Can it be recovered or restored? What kind of penalty and in what amount will compensate the owner of the formerly secret formula or process from the loss of its uniqueness? The author has been involved in legal actions concerning secret formulas in which the claim to be making the product from "the original (name of proprietor) recipe" when that was not, indeed, the case because the defendant claimant did not know the recipe, resulted in substantial money penalties being levied on the defendant. Thus the secret, though NOT revealed, was found to have a very substantial value merely through the threat of its revelation by persons who did not really know it.

Some would believe that the revelation of a secret formula or process of significance, such as that for the concentrate for Coca-Cola, could never be remedied. However, the question arises as to whether the consuming public would believe that a cola made from whatever might be claimed to be that concentrate would really be "their Coca-Cola."

Another way of looking at this issue would be to recognize that Coca-Cola has been in the marketplace since 1886, and if its proprietor had patented the formula (if it were patentable) the patent would have long since expired. It is conceivable that litigation might result in a decision that would conclude that the product should, by now, be generic, and void the right of the Coca-Cola Company to retain its secret.

Ultimately, it would appear that the proprietor who elects to retain a unique formula or process as intellectual property by means of keeping it a secret should recognize that anything known by more than one person is not a secret, and surround the secret with a circle of security that minimizes its likelihood of being revealed.

If You Try and Keep It a Secret, Good Luck!

Defending Against Violation of Employment Contracts

A. Conditions of Contract

A contract is an agreement entered into by two or more persons who possess the following characteristics: (a) the parties to the contract must be competent to enter into a contract; this usually means that they must be at or above a certain age; without inhibition of their civil rights with regard to the matter of the contract; and in possession of their faculties; (b) the purpose of the contract must be legal; (c) consideration, that is, the reciprocal exchange of something of value between the parties, must exist; and (d) the parties must agree to the terms of the contract.

An employment contract is one in which the employee agrees to provide consideration, usually in terms of money, facilities adequate for the employee's performance of the tasks to which he or she will be assigned, and other benefits, in exchange for knowledge and services provided by the employee. The employee, in return, may agree to reveal to the employer but to no other person or persons things that the employee discovers, learns, designs, makes, or otherwise comes into the possession of in connection with or as a result of the employee's employment with the employer. The terms of the contract should be clear and fully understood by both parties.

In a case wherein the employee will be in possession of information that, if revealed to others, would or could damage the business interests of the employer, then a nondisclosure agreement should be a central feature of the employment contract. This agreement should specify explicitly the things the employee was not to reveal and the actions the employer would be entitled to take in the event that the employee violated the agreement.

B. Obligations of the Parties

Both parties have the obligation to act in conformity with the terms of the contract. The contract may be unilaterally violated, in which case the violator becomes liable for civil damages, or bilaterally (or multilaterally) violated, in which case every party to the contract may be subject to liability damages for their failure or, alternatively, due liability damages from others who have violated the contract on their parts. If the act in violation also violates a criminal statute, then criminal proceedings are also called for.

Assuming that the employment contract we are discussing is bilateral with a single employee and single employer and that the employer has acted in good faith in the negotiation with the employee and in providing the agreed-upon things with respect to his obligations to the employee, what are the procedures that the employer should undertake to assure against violation of the employee's part of the contract? These measures should constitute conditions of the contract of which the employee is aware and has agreed to as a condition of entering into the contract.

The employer should undertake to provide relevant security measures for the places in which the employee may work, be called upon to visit, or in which he or she must reside as a condition of employment, so as to minimize the likelihood of purloinment, theft, or illicit removal of work product (either physical or virtual) from those places by the employee. These security measures may and should include elements of surveillance of the workplace, devices that assure that persons entering and leaving secure places are the people who are allowed to enter and leave those places, and record-keeping methods that minimize the likelihood of someone making off with documents, product samples, or other sensitive items.

C. Actions Appropriate in the Event of Apparent Breach of Contract

In the event of an apparent violation of the terms of the employment contract, the employer should undertake such actions as are called for by the normal procedures of investigation to determine whether a violation has taken place. If such a violation is discovered, the employer must act in conformity with the terms of the contract and those aspects of civil and criminal law as might be applicable in the particular case. In some cases, the matter may be settled administratively. In others, litigation or prosecution may be necessary.

The key to effective administration of the preservation of intellectual property by employee contracts is, first, to recruit and investigate likely employees who are known from their prior records to be honest, competent, reliable, and diligent; second, to create employment contracts that are explicit, fair, clearly written, serve to protect the intellectual property involved in the work of the particular employee; and, third, that are consistent with the law and any special conditions (such as the national defense) as might be appropriate. In addition, the process of administration should be conducted by personnel who are trained and experienced in the field and understand the purpose of the employer's business and the roles that the employees in high-security positions play in achieving those objectives.

The ultimate objective of this exercise is to avoid the necessity of litigation or prosecution of employees by discouraging the development of conditions where the incentive for behavior in violation of the employment contract becomes too strong. There is, however, always that possibility. In such a case, the appropriate civil and criminal legal processes should be followed.

Summary

Trade secrets are, for the most part, formulas for assuring that a product will have consistent qualities batch to batch or processes by which ingredients are treated using heat or pressure or some other process to produce the desired product. The ideal secret is something that no one knows. Trade secrets must necessarily be known, in whole or at least in part, by one or several people within the firm in order that the product based on the secret can be produced. Knowledge of a trade secret implies a high degree of trust placed upon an employee. Employee contracts are a way of formalizing the agreements that are implicit in the trust of any employee with all or part of a trade secret by an employer. Contracts have four very specific requirements under the law: the parties to a contract must be competent to enter into the contract; the purpose of the contract must be legal; consideration, the reciprocal exchange of something of value between the parties, must exist; and the parties must agree to the terms of the contract. All parties have the obligation to act in conformity with the terms of the contract. In the event a person violates the terms of the contract, they are certainly subject to civil damages. If the act in violation also violates a criminal law, criminal penalties also apply.

Protecting Intellectual Property Internationally

CHAPTER 9

International Protection of Intellectual Property

The Legal Basis for International Protection of Rights

A. The Presence of Intellectual Property Law

With a few very rare exceptions, each of the some 200 countries in the world today possesses a body of intellectual property rights law. These laws differ from one nation to another, and individuals and firms seeking to do business internationally should be aware that those divisions, subsidiaries, and employees of their firms domiciled in a country will be subject first to its laws and courts in the instance of an intellectual property rights dispute between their firm or any of its elements and any element of the local government, a domestic company of the country in question, or a citizen of the domestic country. Thus, the international business should recognize the necessity of becoming aware of the differences between the laws in their home nation and those of the nations in which they will be doing business as a foreign entity.

B. Forms of National Legal Systems

The legal systems of the various nations fall into five major categories: "code" or "civil" systems based on Roman or Napoleonic law; "common law" systems based on English law; religious systems primarily based on Islamic law; "customary" systems based on local tradition; and hybrid systems usually based on two of the four systems noted above. Of the five, the civil and common law systems account for the greatest shares of world population and gross domestic product. Most of Europe and South America, much of the Far East, and substantial parts of Africa follow various approaches to civil law. Great Britain, Australia, and New Zealand, and most of the United States and Canada (with the exception of Quebec and Louisiana), follow common law. Many of the states of North Africa, the Middle East, and the southern parts of the former Soviet Union follow Islamic law, with small enclaves of customary law appearing here and there in isolated continental regions and on island chains worldwide. As one might expect, the actual bodies of law found in the various areas differ widely and it is better to examine each of them before actually seeking entry to their business world.

The Paris and Berne Conventions and Their Provisions

A. The Treaty Concept: The Paris Convention

In this connection, it is good to recognize the existence of the treaties that have great significance in the administration of intellectual property. The oldest of these is the "Paris Convention for the Protection of Intellectual Property," initially signed in Paris in March of 1883, and still in force today. As of December, 2011, 174 countries share the title of "contracting member." For the purposes of discussion of this treaty, "industrial property" can be taken to mean "patents" and "trademarks." By the terms of this convention, persons—whether juristics or natural—shall enjoy in all the other countries of the convention the advantages that their respective countries' laws grant to nationals. Thus, if a foreigner files for a patent or trademark in another country of the convention, his or her application must be treated the same as that of a domestic applicant and, if the patent or trademark is issued, the owner must similarly be treated as a domestic recipient of the issued document would be treated. Moreover, an applicant for either patent or trademark from one member country of the convention who files an application in another member country of the convention within 6 months (for industrial designs and trademarks) of the initial filing or within 12 months of the initial filing (for patents and utility models) can use the first filing date as the effective filing date for both (or all of the relevant) applications. This "priority right" can be quite effective in protecting the rights for which the patents, trademarks, and other protections are sought.

The Paris Convention is administered by the World Intellectual Property Organization (WIPO) of Geneva, Switzerland.

B. The Berne Convention

The "Berne Convention for the Protection of Literary and Artistic Works," first executed in Berne, Switzerland, in 1886, requires its members to recognize the copyright of works of authors who belong to the members of the Berne Union in the same way as they recognize the rights of authors from their own countries. Even if the work of an author was written in Belgium, for example, if it is published in member-state Austria and copyrighted there, it does not matter where it was written. The Berne Convention, in fact, mandates against a requirement for formal registration in order for a copyright to be effective.

The Berne Convention also provides the basis for the term of copyright to be 50 years after the death of the last living author of a written work, allowing for even longer term at the wish of member countries who desire them. Photographs receive a term of copyright of at least 25 years after the death of the author, while motion pictures are copyrighted for at least 50 years after the first showing of the film. The United States, a latecomer to membership in the Berne Union, has applied a term of 70 years after the death of the last living author to practically all works copyrighted under the convention, making its copyrights among the longest in duration in the world. The Berne Convention, like the Paris Convention, is administered by the World Intellectual Property Organization of Geneva.

The World Trade Organization and the Council for Trade-Related Aspects of Intellectual Property Rights

A newcomer to the field of International Intellectual Property Administration is the World Trade Organization (WTO), founded in 1995 under the Marrakech Agreement and replacing the General Agreement on Tariffs and Trade of 1948. It deals with the regulation of trade between and among membership countries, providing as well a framework for negotiating and formalizing trade agreements. Further, the WTO also provides a dispute resolution process designed to enforce participants to WTO agreements signed by representatives of member governments and ratified by their governments.

The most significant effort on the part of the WTO with respect to Intellectual Property Rights and Administration is its establishment, within its General Council, of the Council for Trade-Related Aspects of Intellectual Property Rights (TRIPS), the purpose of which is to oversee information on intellectual property within the WTO and report on its own activities and work with other organizations in the IPR field. Though it is difficult to say that the Council for TRIPS has accomplished a great deal in the field of intellectual property rights administration, it is safe to say that it has developed communication channels that did not previously exist in the area, and as a result, caused the United States to lengthen its patent duration to 20 years to be consistent with that of other nations.

How Well Have the International Agreements Worked? The China Experience

A. Recent International Allegations of Blatant Trademark Violations (including Trade Dress) Against China

1. History of the Chinese Automobile Industry

   As this author has pointed out in other work in the international sphere, apparently flagrant copying of automotive designs, product shape and appearance, and other trade dress aspects is rampant in some areas of the globe, especially but not exclusively where nations are not signatories of the Berne or Paris Convention. Though a signatory of the Paris Convention, and a member of the World Trade Organization since 2002, China is one of the countries that has been accused of producing vehicles by copying the appearance of automobiles and other vehicles made and trademarked in other nations.

   The first automobile factory to begin production in China was the First Automobile Works, opened in 1956. Most vehicular production between then and the mid-1980s was concentrated in light- and medium-duty trucks based on Russian GAZ models. Indeed, in 1985, Chinese output of automobiles was only 5,200 units.[1]

2. The Years of Importation

In light of their inability to meet demand in the domestic market-place, China first turned to the importation of foreign vehicles, bringing in some 350,000 units in 1985 alone.[2] In subsequent years, China resorted to joint-venture arrangements for the man-ufacture of foreign makes in China with Volkswagen (Shanghai Automotive Industry Corporation and a new First Automobile Works), and Citroen (Dongfeng Motor Corporation). Three smaller joint ventures also appeared: Beijing Automotive Industry (Hyundai Motors, DaimlerChrysler: Jeep), Guangzhou Automobile Industry Group (Peugeot, later Honda and also Toyota), and Tianjin Automotive Industry (Daihatsu).

Additional firms such as Chang'an Motors, Changhe, and Hafei Motor entered the market on their own, emerging from China's defense industry. They were followed by BYD Auto, Brilliance China Auto, Chery Automobile, and Changfeng Auto, for-merly state-owned firms. New privately owned companies such as Geely Automobile and Great Wall Motors entered the market as well.

3. Production Increasing Geometrically Beginning in the 1980s and Continuing till today

Chinese automobile production skyrocketed in the later 1980s and continued to grow in leaps and bounds during the decades of the 1990s and 2000s, reaching an output of 18 million units in year 2010.[3] The going was not entirely clear, however, with Chinese makers being accused of copying the designs of foreign automakers. The leader of those accused with producing copy-cat models was BYD, which has been alleged to have copied cars from Lexus,[4] Toyota,[5] Honda,[6] Mercedes-Benz,[7] and Porsche.[8]

General Motors went so far as to file suit in China against Chery for the design features of their Model QQ (BBC News, May 9, 2005) but after 2 years of moving from venue to venue, ultimately dropped the charges against the Chinese company. Among those charges were that many of the body components of the QQ were identical to those of the Daewoo Matiz and would fit without alteration (Daewoo is a GM associate firm). The visual similarity of the CHERY and CHEVY names were alleged to be a less-than-subtle effort on the part of the Chinese automobile maker to trade on the colloquial name for the Chevrolet product from General Motors.

FIAT, in turn, sued Great Wall Motor Company claiming that Great Wall's "Jing Ling" was a copy of the FIAT Panda. A Turin court supported FIAT's position, but Chinese courts have not been so understanding.

Finally, Mercedes-Benz has sued Shuanghuan on the grounds that their "Noble" was entirely too much like the Smart "Fortwo." Again, an Italian court supported Mercedes' position, forbidding the showing of the Noble at the Bologna Car Show. A Greek judge ruled against Mercedes' position, clearing the car for sale in the Greek market, the grounds being, essentially, that the car which Mercedes sought to impede entry of into the Greek market was not the Noble that they claimed was infringing on the Smart in question.[9]

Recalling that The Peoples' Republic of China is a member of the World Trade Organization and a signatory of the Paris Convention, with 45 automobile manufacturing companies of its own,[10] does it have a justification for manufacturing identical or near-identical copies of vehicles made elsewhere, particularly when one considers that a number of foreign makes, such as Buick and Volkswagen, are manufactured under license in China? The Chinese have, in fact, made the defense that copying the best of what exists is historically and culturally an approach taken by newly emerging nations seeking to bootstrap their economies in particular areas. Most examples of such behavior, such as Japan's emergence from the Shogunate in the second half of the nineteenth century and Russia's industrial development before and immediately after World War II, are now long past and were not undertaken by nations leading the world in production of the products they were accused of copying nor were they signatories of treaties explicitly designed to prevent such behavior.

Summary

Most of the world's nations possess a body of intellectual property rights law. The majority of the legal systems extant are either "code" systems (sometimes called "civil" systems) based on Roman or Napoleonic law or "common law" systems based on British law. There are, in addition, systems based on religious beliefs, systems based on local tradition, and hybrid systems based on two or more of the above five. Most of the world's major nations are either common law or civil states. Each nation's laws differ from those of other nations, so the protection of intellectual property on an international basis depends upon treaties—agreements signed by many nations to handle actions according to certain procedures and rules—and the presence of organizations to administer the treaties and other agreements by all or some of the participating nations that supplement the treaties. The major treaties affecting intellectual property rights are the Paris Convention of 1883 (as amended) and the Berne Convention of 1886 (also as amended). These treaties are administered by the World Intellectual Property Organization of Geneva, Switzerland. Other organizations that are involved in the administration of intellectual property rights are The World Trade Organization and the Council for Trade Related Aspects of Intellectual Property Rights. Despite the efforts of these organizations, the behavior of some nations that are their members has been less than conforming in recent years. China's automobile manufacturers, who among them became the world's largest makers of automobiles in 2010, have been sued or accused of copying vehicles by Lexus, Toyota, Honda, Mercedes-Benz, Porsche, General Motors, and FIAT. A Chinese official responded to a compendium of these accusations with the rejoinder that China was simply acquiring technology from the rest of the world to build an industry just like the Soviet Union did after World War II. China, however, is a member of the World Trade Organization and a signatory of the Paris Convention.

CHAPTER 10

Creating Intellectual Property Rights From a Standing Start: Russia Since 1992

How and Why Do You Create a Field of Legal Jurisprudence Overnight?

A. If We're Russia, Where Do We Begin?

To understand why it is important to look at the behavior of the Russian Federation with respect to intellectual property, it is necessary to realize that the USSR, the predecessor nation to the federation, espoused a communist economic and political philosophy for over 70 years before its collapse in the 1990s. The orientation of the Soviet Union toward intellectual property was that such property belonged to the state and not to any individual. The demise of the former nation and the embrace of a market-driven economy by the new one mandated a recognition that intellectual property was now to be, for the most part, private property and a body of law had to be crafted to facilitate the change.

In most industrialized nations, the concept and body of intellectual property laws is well into its fourth century of development and testing. The Russian Federation, however, has created and implemented an entirely new body of intellectual property law since the collapse of the Soviet Union in 1992. As American and other Western firms work with the Russian Federation as a supplier and customer, they must recognize that the new nation has struggled to abandon a legal philosophy denying the existence of intellectual property in favor of a new set of intellectual property laws recognizing and favoring private development and ownership of such property. This chapter examines the new Russian intellectual property laws and certain holdovers of Russian behavior since the collapse of the Soviet union and suggests adaptations that citizens and businesses of historically non-Communist nations should make when dealing with similar entities in the Russian Federation. It assumes familiarity with Russian history, language, and geography. A preliminary caution to domestic firms is that they should retain experienced legal counsel to deal with negotiations and contracts with Russian business interests.

The Russian Federation: Who Are These People?

A. A Description of the Nation

The Russian Federation is the successor nation to the Russian Soviet Federated Socialist Republic (RSFSR), which ceased to exist in January 1992. The new federation is a republic and federal rule-of-law state that claims a judicial commitment to the principles of democracy. The nation is known both as the Russian Federation and Russia and the names are used interchangeably. The Russian Federation is a member of the Commonwealth of Independent States (CIS), which includes ten nations that are not members of the Russian Federation. Together, they seek to develop an economic community coordinating economic policy to ultimately result in a free market system.

By the terms of its constitution, the Russian Federation includes republics, territories, regions, federal cities, an autonomous region, and autonomous areas, each of which is an equal subject of the federation. They total 84 entities. Each republic in the federation has its own constitution and legislative, judicial, and executive branches much as do the states of the USA, and possesses a substantial degree of political and economic independence. The other entities in the federation are somewhat less independent than the republics, with individual charters and legislation but not a separate constitution (Constitution of the Russian Federation, Sec. 1, Ch. 1, Art. 5 et seq.)

The terms of the Russian Federal Constitution and federal legislation preempt the laws of federation member entities when the two conflict. The federal government possesses executive, judiciary, and legislative branches. The executive is led by the president, who is officially chief of state. Its other members are the chairman of the government (head of government or prime minister); deputy chairman of the government; and other ministers, all of whom together comprise the cabinet. There are other specialized branches of the executive such as the presidential administration (provides staff and policy assistance to the president) and the Security Council (coordinates matters of national security and reports to the president).

The judicial branch of the Federation government includes the Constitutional Court, the Supreme Court, the Supreme Court of Arbitration, and the Prosecutor-General's Office. Judges for all courts are appointed for life by the Federation Council on the nomination of the president. The Russian legislature consists of two houses, the Duma and the Federal Council. Together they are called the Federal Assembly. The Duma has 450 seats, elected on the basis of population from the various entities of the federation. (This section is taken from the Constitution of the Russian Federation, in gross.)

The Russian Legal System

The Russian legal system is a civil (code) system, which provides for judicial review (but not amendment) of statutory law. The civil system of law does not allow for law to be made in the courtroom but only by statute, and previous judicial decisions by themselves cannot be cited as precedent for subsequent decisions. Judicial review is designed to assure that the laws themselves are consistent with the thrust of the code in which they are embodied. Thus, a law may be declared unconstitutional by the appropriate court, but interpretation of law as to meaning is reserved solely to the Supreme Court of the Federation.

The Russian judiciary is composed of three parts: first, there is the regular court system (the courts of general jurisdiction) with its capstone being the Supreme Court; second, there are the courts of arbitration capped by the Supreme Court of Arbitration; and finally, there is the Constitutional Court, a single unit with no other courts in its ambit. Each of these three elements of the judiciary has its own subject-matter jurisdiction. The Constitutional Court, for example, is the court of constitutional review, which is its sole area of responsibility, and it is the only court in the federation with the authority to nullify a statute by declaring it unconstitutional. The Constitutional Court's declaration of a law to be unconstitutional is the only instance in which a Russian court may change an existing statute.

The courts of arbitration handle disputes between business entities. The Supreme Court of Arbitration is the highest court of appeal in this area of law. If, however, a legal dispute involves a business entity and at least one private citizen who is not involved in the business activities that gave rise to the dispute, then the courts of general jurisdiction are responsible for the adjudication.

The Supreme Court of the Federation cannot nullify legislation, but it can interpret legislation as to meaning. The Supreme Court also guides the courts of general jurisdiction on specific matters of law and procedure. Decisions on these matters by the Supreme Court bind the lower courts and administrative agencies and also state officials who deal with the matters decided by the Supreme Court.

Intellectual Property in Russia: History of the Issue

The Constitution of the Russian Federation[1] replaces the Constitution of the Russian Soviet Federated Socialist Republic of 1978. As such, it is a far more democratic document on its face than is its predecessor. It has no fewer than 47 articles[2] dealing with the human rights guaranteed by the document.

The history of Russian intellectual property rights follows the general Western–European developmental history of such rights, albeit lagging the thrust of similar legislation by perhaps a century. Czar Alexander I signed the "Manifesto on the Privileges for Inventions and Discoveries in the Arts and Sciences" on June 17, 1812. Subsequently, laws were passed such that, as the twentieth century approached, the "Regulations on Privileges for Inventions and Improvements" of May 20, 1896, included most of the components of a modern patent system, such as enablement, novelty, and utility requirements, and a 15-year exclusive patent term.[3]

Following the Revolution of 1917, the Russian political and legal environment changed almost overnight. Gone was the Empire of the Czar and its capitalist structure. The new Soviet Republic featured a regulated, planned economy with subsidized production, a complete prohibition of private enterprise, and abolition of private ownership of property. The state now owned all but the most basic forms of property.

The aftermath of the Bolshevik overthrow revealed to the new Russian administration the problems inherent in a truly communist state and in 1921 the "New Economic Policy" was initiated, bringing back free enterprise and a market economy. During the period of the New Economic Policy, which coincided with the primacy of V. I. Lenin as head of state, the terms of the 1896 law were apparently considered to be reinstated, though without repassage.[4] With the end of the New Economic Policy on the death of Lenin in 1928, efforts were set afoot by the new government dominated by Joseph Stalin to bring intellectual property rights policy into synchronicity with other Russian policy, resulting in the passage, in 1931, of the "Regulations on Inventions and Technological Improvements." This statute abolished private ownership of intellectual property rights. Instead of the inventor or other rights holder in due course of intellectual property rights being able to control their disposition, the state became the rights holder and the inventor received a nominal remuneration and a "certificate of invention" for his or her work.[5] This system remained in place for over 50 years until the mid-1980s when the instability of Russian politics and the economy finally induced Mikhail Gorbachev to reinstate some forms of private enterprise and relieve the strictures of the planned economy.

The continued instability of the socialist state after Gorbachev's action soon became obvious and by 1991 resulted in the failure of the Russian political system. It also became obvious that the pre-Soviet Union intellectual property laws were untenable. It took until 1992 to confect a new set of laws regulating the disposition of intellectual property rights. Those laws, embodying a number of amendments, remain in effect in substance today and will be discussed at length herein.

The 1992 Reforms: The Legal Framework of Modern Russian Intellectual Property Legislation

Remember that the underlying structure of the Russian legal system is the Legal Code, which possesses both civil and criminal components. In the courts, arguments must be based on the determination of the facts in a case, which are examined for merit by the court in the context of relevant law. Findings of courts in other jurisdictions concerning similar cases may *not* be used as the basis for argument or decision in new cases. In other words, the use of precedent set by rulings in earlier cases, and the resultant recasting of the law by judges known as Common Law, is not allowed under the Russian system. It was realized shortly after the collapse of the Soviet Union that intellectual property, in the new, non-Communist Federation, required regulation recognizing its new status. The major provisions of the resulting body of legislation are embodied in the five statutes that follow.

1. The Patent Law of the Russian Federation of September 23, 1992, amended February 2003, in force January 1, 2004
   The Russian Federal Institute of Industrial Patents (Rospatent) administers this law, its successor, and the other laws that this section describes. The English language translations and abstracts in use here appear to be correct in detail with respect to the original language and meaning of those laws. These laws have been amended and many of their provisions replaced in the effort to create conformity with the Agreement on Trade-Related Aspects of Intellectual Property Rights and secure for Russia membership in the World Trade Organization. They do, nonetheless, differ somewhat from the laws of other nations. Comparisons between Russian and U.S. laws made here are made on the assumption that most readers of this document will be native speakers of Russian or English and that such comparisons will be relevant to them.

   The Russian Patent Law of 1992 recognizes three things that qualify for patent protection: inventions, utility models, and industrial designs. By definition, inventions are new, novel, and useful applications of science or engineering. Generally, they improve in some way the means in which something is made, processed, or handled. The term of invention patents under the 1992 law runs for 20 years from the date on which application for them is filed and is ordinarily not extensible. Patents on medications, pesticides, and agrichemicals requiring government permission for use (by the

Russian equivalent of the U.S. Food and Drug Administration) may be extended in the sense that the term of 20 years begins to run when the first permission for use is granted.

Utility model patents, which are patents on technical solutions relating to a device (such as improved control systems for machinery and the like) run for 5 years from the date of application and are extensible under certain circumstances for 3 additional years. Industrial design patents, which apply to aesthetic presentations that define the overall appearance and identity of a product, run for 10 years from the date of application and may be extended for 5 years. By contrast, U.S. Patent Law recognizes invention patents (with a term of 20 years) and plant patents with a similar term and design patents (with a 14-year term) and allows no extension except when the application is contested and the applicant prevails, in which case the patent runs for 20 years from the date the patent is granted and retroactively to the date of application (35 USC 156(F)1(a) and cases).

Both Russian and U.S. Patent Laws provide for secret patents of inventions which involve issues of state security. Under Russian law, neither utility models nor industrial designs may be patented secretly. The Russian Patent Law specifically prohibits patenting computer software, nor may plant varieties or animal breeds be patented. Also barred from patent are the topology of integrated circuits and devices not in the public interest or which result in the abrogation of human rights or are immoral in purpose.

2. The Law of the Russian Federation of September 23, 1992, on Trademarks, Service Marks, and Appellations of Origin of Goods, amended December 11, 2002, in force December 27, 2002
Trademarks, which this law classes into the subsets "trademarks" and "service marks," may be "words, figures, three dimensional or other signs in any colors or combinations of colors" whose purpose is to identify the product, the service, or the holder of the mark so that they will not be confused with other products, services, or mark holders. By Russian law, trademarks achieve protection *only* by registration with the government. Required regulation is consistent with Russia's civil law. The common law custom of protection by

"first and continuous use" does not apply. In Russia, marks must be registered by a legal entity and a natural person, which may be one and the same. These then become the "right-holder" of the mark or the "mark-holder." Use of the trademark or any "confusingly similar mark" by anyone other than the right holder is illegal.

Trademarks may be fanciful or straightforward, applied to the product itself or the service related to the mark, or to the firm or individual holding the mark. Proposed trademarks will be denied coverage if they are (a) words, terms, or other signs in common use to designate that class of good, (b) words, terms, or other signs in general use as part of the language, or (c) descriptive or depictive of the product's function.

3. The Law of the Russian Federation of July 9, 1993 on Copyright and Ancillary Rights, amended December 11, 2002, in force July 23, 2003

This law lays the foundation for protection of creative works of a written, carved, painted, played, sung, photographed, or phono-grammatic nature within the federation. The "author" of such a work must be a natural person but may be a group of natural persons working in concert. The method of production of the work may be "objective" or "virtual." Twenty-eight kinds of works are specifically covered as are 11 specific classes of work. The duration of copyright in the Russian Federation is the lifetime of the author plus 70 years or 70 years for a posthumously published work, the same as in the United States. The Russian law provides for a different class of copy-right for performances, which calls for the use of the symbol of a "P" in a circle rather than the © used for other copyrighted works.

4. The Law of the Russian Federation of September 23, 1992, on the Legal Protection of Computer Programs and Databases, amended December 24, 2002, in force January 7, 2003

5. The Law of the Russian Federation of September 23, 1992, on the Legal Protection of the Topologies of Integrated Circuits, amended prepass July 9, 2002, in force October 1, 2002

These laws, as their names imply, cover proprietary rights in new technologies. The Russians have elected to handle these areas in new legislation rather than attempt to shoehorn them into legislation designed to deal with more established areas of intellectual property rights.

The first of these two laws has, among its other provisions, language that extends copyright protection to databases and certain types of computer programs. The second law both protects the design of certain types of electrical circuits and closes a loophole in previous legislation that provided no remedy for companies whose proprietary chip designs had been stolen.

Loopholes in the 1990s Statutes

At first blush, the body of law created by the legal community of the Russian Federation in 1992–1994 to handle intellectual property rights after approximately 60 years of denial of their existence seems remarkably consistent and up to date until one realizes that the Russian legal scholars had access to something like three centuries of the development of such laws in other jurisdictions (and in their own prior to the 1917 Revolution).

The language of the Russian laws is clear, concise, and seemingly enforceable. Their separation of matters such as databases, computer software, and integrated circuit topology from the more traditional areas of the field is evidence of recognition of the newness and still-growing nature of these subjects. However, the writing of laws to control the administration of a class of property the existence of which was denied for so very long did not necessarily mean that the mind-sets of the people charged with administering those laws, many of whom remained as residue from the prior bureaucracy, would change.

The Apparatchiks Versus the Law

The Communist administration had created in Russia, during its years of presence as the Soviet, a bureaucracy noted for its inefficiency, corruption, and the prevalence of "apparatchiks." Analogous in roles to the "career civil servants" of the West, these members of the Communist Party elite operated on a "what's in it for me" basis. Their positions were derived from party membership rather than training or skills.

Among the things they believed were "in it for them" were positions in the bureaucracy for their children, so that by the late 1980s some bureaus of the Russian government were staffed largely, particularly in the middle-management ranks, with apparatchiks who were themselves the children and grandchildren of earlier "apparatchiks." Thus one might expect there to be a certain antipathy, at best, on the part of government employees to the enforcement of the new laws. After all, in the "good old days" a successful inventor only got an invention certificate and a modest sum of money.

Why should such inventors or, analogously, newly minted business successes now get a monopoly on their creativity for 20 years or more? Such was the thinking of the "apparatchiks in place" of the Russian government. It might be theorized, therefore, that enforcement of the new laws by a bureaucracy with such a mind-set might not be as avid or dedicated as one might expect from the rigor of their confection.

In the post-1992, pre-2007 period, this was indeed the case. Russia appeared on the Special 301 Priority Watch List of the Special 301 Report (an annual review that examines in detail the adequacy and effectiveness of intellectual property rights protection in 87 countries and places those of dubious quality on the Watch List) of the U.S. Trade Representative (USTR) beginning in 1997.[6]

Illegal copying of Compact (CD) and Video (DVD) Disks

The USTR estimated that 80 percent of the Russian market for digital video disks (DVDs) and 66 percent of the music compact disks (CDs) sold there in 1996 were pirated.[7] It was estimated that as many as 52 plants having a capacity to produce as many as 450 million disks operated on Russian soil. Of the 23 plants discovered to have produced pirated copies of copyrighted disks, at least 8 were located on Restricted Access Regime Enterprise (RARE) territories owned or leased by the Russian government, usually former military bases to which access by civil authorities is severely restricted.[8] Moreover, the same authors report that pirated copies of optical disks have appeared in 27 countries outside Russia.

Illegal Copying of Pharmaceuticals

Pharmaceutical copying has also been a major source of intellectual property abuse within Russia. As early as April, 2002, the *Saint Petersburg (Russia) Times* quoted industry sources as saying that 12 percent of all prescription, over the counter, and even vitamin products sold in Russia were counterfeit and predicted that the quantity could reach 25 percent within 2 years.[9]

The European Union, in its 2006 survey of EU businesses concerning their experience with intellectual property rights issues outside the EU in 2005, identifies Russia, second only to China, as one of the five countries (along with Ukraine, Chile, and Turkey) with high levels of production, transit, and consumption of counterfeit goods who need to step up their efforts to tackle serious deficiencies.[10]

The 2006 Version of Title Seven of the Civil Code

The 1992 statutes anticipated the larger body of new Russian law by 14 years, the time between their passage and the completion by the Federal Assembly of the larger Civil Code of the Russian Federation, of which they were initially anticipated to become a part. In the interim, the laws were in force and were amended as necessary to plug egregious loopholes. As the year 2006 developed, Part Four of the Civil Code of the Russian Federation approached completion. This title, the last of the Code, was designed to be a comprehensive treatment of intellectual property rights, encompassing the existing body of law and correcting, en bloc, the flaws which had become apparent in 14 years of administration.

Part Four introduced amplifications and some diminutions of the terms of the early-1990s laws. As its adoption loomed, the Coalition for Intellectual Property Rights (CIPR) conducted a survey of Russian Intellectual Property Rights owners in Russia to measure their opinions about the new legislation. The findings were not promising. Seventy percent of those responding were negative about the proposed changes while 25 percent were positive. Sixty-seven percent said they believed the proposal would reduce the effectiveness of IP enforcement in Russia. Sixty-eight percent agreed with the statement "It is of the utmost importance to strictly enforce existing legislation" rather than make changes to the IP laws already in force. Peter Necarsulmer, president of CIPR, summed up the results of the survey by saying "Russian and international rights holders are clearly saying that … they are satisfied with the legal basis of Russia's IP regime so now is not the time for major mid-course changes. The government and the IP community should zero in on fighting counterfeiting, piracy and wide-spread IP rights abuse."[11]

Nonetheless, President Putin signed Part Four of the Civil Code into law. No sooner had this been done than the president met with the Russian Federal Government Intellectual Property Rights (RFG IPR) Experts Council and it was agreed that the Duma and the drafters of the law would meet to amend it during the Duma session of Spring 2007. The result would go into force on January 1, 2008. By this time, serious pressure was on Russia to qualify for membership in the World Trade Organization and to comply with The Agreement on Trade-Related Aspects of Intellectual Property Rights.

Some of the problems to be addressed during the Duma session were examined by CIPR. In brief, the issues present in the unamended Part Four signed in December 2006 were summarized by CIPR as follows:[12]

a. There is a lack of a uniform standard for infringement. (Trademarks, company names, domain names, etc., are handled differently.)

b. Domain names receive overbroad protection (being given senior status even over trademarks).

c. Protection of commercial designations and company names are overbroad (also, in some instances, becoming senior over trademarks.)

d. Overbroad protection of Soviet-era marks. (Such marks were grandfathered in under the new law even if identical to marks legally claimed under the 1992 law.)

e. Well-known marks are insufficiently well protected.

   1. Geographic Indications receive absolute priority over trademarks in violation of TRIPS and the 2005 WTO Protocol.

   2. No provision is made for opposition to trademark and geographic indications prior to registration.

   3. Rospatent procedures are not transparent. (Pending trademark applications are not published prior to registration and public access to applicant files is restricted.)

4. The provisions concerning trademark licensing and franchising are excessively complex, to wit:
    i. The concept of quality control far exceeds international norms.
    ii. The legislation imposes burdensome requirements regarding the content of trademark licenses.
    iii. Trademark licenses must be mandatorily recorded against the registration of the licensed mark, a burdensome and expensive practice.
    iv. The new law prohibits unregistered marks being licensed as parts of a franchise.
  f. There is no provision for fair use of trademarks.
  g. No specific effort is made to remedy the existing problems under Russian law concerning counterfeiting and piracy.

Part Four of the Current Russian Civil Code (The 2008 Statutes)

Part Four of the Russian Civil Code as placed in effect on January 1, 2008, supersedes the Patent Law of 1992; the Law on Trademarks, Service Marks, and Appellation of Origin of 1992; the Law on Copyright and Related Rights of 1993, which were discussed earlier in this work; and the Law on the Provisions on a Firm of 1927, Article 138-139 of the Russian Civil Code, not otherwise mentioned herein. Amendments were also made to those articles of the Civil Code having to do with franchising (Federal Law No. 230-FZ "Civil Code of the Russian Federation, Part Four" of December 18, 2007).

The Russian Criminal Code, Article 180, was also changed to provide for stiffer jail sentences and monetary penalties (the former maximum of 10,000 Rubles was increased to 5 million Rubles) for trademark infringement along with double indemnity of twice the value of the infringing goods, and the new Article 146 now allows jail terms of up to 6 years for copyright infringement, making this a serious offense under Russian law.

With respect to patents, the most significant changes under Part Four have been the increase in the terms of utility model patents from 5 years to 10, and of industrial design patents from 10 years to 15. The overall substance of the law of patents, however, remains unchanged.

The new version of Article 138 of the Civil Code, unlike its predecessor, provides an extensive list of intellectual property objects. In some cases, particular things, such as commercial designations, are recognized as intellectual property rights for the first time.

The new Part Four applies in some respect to both copyrights and trademarks. The new law simplifies the regulation of license agreements in both contexts. It subjects license agreements to a detailed list of requirements, the net result of which is to clarify the meaning of such agreements in the specific. The licensor is no longer required to supervise the quality control of the licensee but may do so if he or she so wishes. In addition, the grounds for refusal of a trademark have been made more specific with respect to the issue of confusion but broader with respect to other issues.

The conflict between the right of superiority formerly granted to domain names over trademarks and the usual practice of trademark superiority has been resolved in the current Part Four. Rospatent does retain, however, some rights of restriction of public inspection of trademark applications under Items 1–7 of Article 1483 of the Civil Code.

The new Part Four of the Civil Code is a much clearer document. The influence of the desire of the Russian Federation to qualify for membership in the WTO and membership in the TRIPS Agreement is apparent.

A. Is this the beginning of a real shift toward acceptance of the law?

Even the thrust of recent Russian legal proceedings seems to show an increased interest in upholding the new law. In November 2007, in anticipation of the implementation of Part Four, four managers at Brynsalov-A, a Russian pharmaceutical firm, were charged with the use of trademarks owned by several Western pharmaceutical companies. Each of them faces a prison term of up to 6 years if convicted.[13]

In a second case, the Moscow region Arbitration Court ruled that Lukoil's trademark was illegally used by a gasoline filling station in the Moscow area. Observers consider this to mark the beginning of a trend of successful enforcement actions in the arbitration courts.[14]

B. An Interesting Anecdote

Quite interestingly, one of the most well-known products to emerge from the old Soviet Union—some 60 years ago—the Kalashnikov automatic rifle, originally named the Automat Kalashnikov 47

(AK-47), but very soon replaced with the more cheap-to-make but equally effective AKM, became the subject of a threatened trademark or patent action by the Russian government. Novosti, the Russian news organization, reported in 2008 that total production of the Kalashnikov worldwide has exceeded 100 million units, but that Russia receives few royalties for current production from the some 47 countries who use the weapon as their military standard. The Russian point of view seems to be that they are entitled to payments for Kalashnikovs made outside Russia. Most recently, noises along this line were being made by Dmitry Rogozin, the Russian ambassador to NATO.

The reason for Rogozin's assertion, despite the fact that Russia's former Soviet-bloc allies turned out most of the knock-off AKMs, seems to stem from the fact that the U.S. Pentagon purchased the AK-based rifles with which they supplied Iraqi and Afghani security forces from non-Russian sources. Any patent on the design, had one ever existed, would have expired in 1967. Since it is highly dubious that many Russian Kalashnikovs bore trademarks and it is moreover true that Russia insisted on production and adoption of the weapon by her former Warsaw Pact allies, any patent or trademark infringement claim is, on its face, specious. It does, however, reveal that the Russians have now at least developed a grasp of the concept behind intellectual property.[15]

C. Can Evolutionary Processes Really be Accelerated or is Russia Pedaling as Fast as It Can?

Twenty years ago, the Soviet Union, the nation many Americans thought of as "The Evil Empire," celebrated its seventieth anniversary as a Communist country. Three years later, the nation emerged from political discord and instability as the Russian Federation, a new, non-Communist nation that modeled its organization on that of the non-British-empire nations of Western Europe. Old habits and political institutions do not die overnight, however, so the new nation began a process of adaptation that included the gradual replacement of one bureaucracy—that of the Communist Party apparatchiks—for another, based more or less on the professional civil-service class of the West. The process began slowly because of the persistence in the bureaucracy of the same people who had been there before the change, but it began.

On its face, the new Russian Federation appeared to outside interests to be a desirable market for goods and services. With an area of just over 17 million square kilometers and a population estimated to be approximately 150 million (just slightly more than its pre-World War II population of 140 million) in 1995,[16] it had been, for a number of years, substantially closed to trade with the West because the Ruble had been a "blocked currency" that did not exchange in the open market. Thus, trade with the Soviet Union, particularly by U.S. interests, had been a barter arrangement of goods for goods. The Russians, beginning in 1974, provided American merchants with vodka and received in return American Pepsi-Cola.[17] Thus, trade was stifled unless an explicit agreement of the worth of products could be stated in the worth of the other products for which those were to be exchanged. The risk of trade with Russia, however, beyond erring in the estimation of the value of the traded goods, was minimal.

The appearance of the Russian Federation, however, began to change things. Direct foreign investment by the USA and other outside interests became, despite the risk of political instability in the new nation, at least worth considering. The new laws, despite their defects, at least recognized the idea of intellectual property and made some attempt to sanction it along with the other property rights of individuals (including corporations.)

At this time, trade with Russia is facilitated by the abandonment of currency blockage and a market for Russian currency outside Russia. The Ruble, at this writing, is quoted at R29.84 to the U.S. dollar.[18] In addition, the Russians seem to have become much more interested in enforcing the intellectual property laws, as evidenced by prosecutions such as those cited above.

The adaptive process of the past two decades has made the Russian Federation a much less risky place for Russians and foreigners to seek to profit from their possession of intellectual property rights. The system is not perfect, but then what legal system is. It is still, and will always be, the creature of the people who administer, interpret, and enforce the laws and regulations of which it is composed. When the political atmosphere, economic conditions, and the government itself are stable and positively oriented, risk to property rights is minimal. When any or all of these fall into question, the risk increases.

In sum, over the past 20 years, initially, laws were changed. Then people began to change, but slowly, to reflect the new philosophy embodied in those laws. Time passed. It was realized that further legislative change was required. The laws were amended. People changed a bit more. More time passed. The laws existed, but enforcement was spotty and still plagued by the persistence of old attitudes. People changed some more. It was realized that different laws were required. Time passed. The new laws went into effect. The question now is: "How much more change, both legislative and psychological, will have to take place before Russia can be said to have achieved its proclaimed goal of being a major free-market power in the twenty-first century?"

D. So Where Are We Now and How, in Sum, Have Things Changed?
The most recent formal analysis of the risks and rewards of doing business in Russia appeared in January 2011.[19] Prepared by Steven Kelly at VMConsult, a respected international business consulting firm in Moscow, this report acknowledged Russia's leadership position as an energy producer providing over 30 percent of the crude oil, 7.9 percent of the hard coal, and over 30 percent of the natural gas imported by the European Union. The report also lauded Russia's planned 13 trillion Ruble (about US $460 billion) investment in transport infrastructure planned for 2010–2015.

Russia has also become a leading producer of ferrous, nonferrous, and precious metals entering the world market. Metals and metal products are now Russia's second largest group of exports. While nonprecious metals production is still largely in government hands, production of gold and silver is in the hands of private enterprise.

Retailing in Russia continues to grow in every sector and Russia is now the fastest-growing market for luxury goods. The Russian automotive industry continues to grow, though automobile ownership is only about one-third the level of other European countries.

Do Risks Remain and How Bad Are They?

According to the VMConsult Report, although Russia has progressed significantly since 1992, certain risks do still exist in the present and should be considered by foreign investors.

1. Corruption, the operation of the legal system, questions as to the independence of the judiciary from the political arena, red tape, and customs formalities are still issues growing out of the persistent bureaucracy of Russia. These enduring problems increase transaction costs of any venture into the Russian market and thus are essential considerations that must be resolved before successful Russian investment can be made.

2. The dearth of Russian-speaking residents in most European and American countries and the relatively few Russians who speak English remain problems, though some improvement has been made on both sides of the aisle.

3. The Russian government has become relatively stable, but it is relatively young and has been known to make U-turns in policy, sometimes even attacking the very involvement by foreign interests that it formerly encouraged.

4. Russian banks are reluctant to lend money, especially to foreign business interests, loan rates are usually significantly higher than those of Western banks, and the payout terms are shorter. Thus, finding capital for large, long-term projects can be difficult. The presence in Russia of banks such as HSBC, Barclays, and Raiffelsen has improved the situation, but small and medium-sized businesses continue to have capital acquisition difficulties. In addition, the custom of using tax evasion as a method of increasing cash flow practiced by some Russian firms complicates the legal acquisition of loanable funds by outsiders.

5. Finding a suitable business partner in Russia troubles a large number of outside would-be investors. Wal-Mart closed its Russian office in 2011 after being unable, after several years of unsuccessful search, to find a Russian partner with which it would feel comfortable.

Russia and the West: A Brief Summation of the Process of Change

The year 2011 drew to a close with the Russian Federation and the United States of America still on speaking terms and Eastern and Western Europe, despite their overall financial difficulties, now at least marginally comfortable with the idea of living on one continent. We can only hope that it will remain that way and, hopefully, continue to improve.

Summary

The Russian Soviet Federated Socialist Republic (RSFSR), after nearly 70 years in place as the government of Russia and a number of associated states, collapsed and was replaced by the Russian Federation. The new Russian Federation abandoned the Communist philosophy of its predecessor, the abandonment creating the necessity for recognition of the existence of intellectual property rights on the part of citizens of the federation, rights that were denied under the Soviet. The new government, therefore, was forced to create a new body of laws reflective of its new philosophy. The Duma (legislature) diligently went to work, and by October 1992, new patent, copyright, and trademark laws were in place. Though the new laws, at first blush, seemed to be clear, concise, and enforceable, suffered from a number of flaws. The major flaw was not in the confection of the laws, but the necessity for their enforcement. For almost 70 years, the Russian government had been in the hands of people whose main qualification was not ability or dedication, but simply membership in the Communist Party. These "apparatchiks," as they were known, ran the government on a "what's in it for me?" basis. Some of the things that were considered to be "in it" for them were the proceeds from now-illegal copying of pre-recorded compact (CD) and digital video (DVD) disks, often produced in government-owned facilities. Also copied were pharmaceuticals of various sorts, estimated to account for 12 per cent of all pharmaceuticals made in Russia. The penalties provided in the 1992 statutes were relatively light and enforcement not a high priority of the government bureaucracy, so it was realized that changes in both areas were necessary. By 2008, major changes in the 1992 laws had been created, resulting in a new Part Four of the Civil Code. Article 180 of the Criminal Code was changed to create stiffer jail sentences and higher money penalties for violations. New, more specific definitions were provided for intellectual property objects by Article 138 of the Civil Code. In addition, Russian enforcement organizations have begun to aggressively police infringements of intellectual property rights.

Notes

Chapter 1

1. Her Majesty's Patent Office, now the Intellectual Property Office of the United Kingdom (2000).
2. The Patent Office of the European Union (Europäisches Patentamt) (1997).
3. Constitution of the United States of America, Art. I, Sec. 8, Cl. 8.
4. Ladas and Parry (n.d.).
5. Blake (2004).
6. Pollard and Redgrave (1976).
7. The Intellectual Property Office of the United Kingdom (n.d.).
8. Swarbrick (2003).
9. McKinney Engineering Library, University of Texas (n.d.).
10. Tabber's Temptations (n.d.).
11. Ibid, p. 2.
12. *The Trade-Mark Cases* (1879).
13. Coca-Cola Company (2011).
14. http://inventors.about.com/library/inventors/blcrackerjacks.htm

Chapter 2

1. Quinn, Gene "The Cost of Obtaining a Patent in the United States", at http://ipwatchdog.com/2011/01/28
2. http://smallbusiness.findlaw.com/trademark/trademark-registration/state-trademark-information
3. http://tess.2.uspto.gov/netahtm/tidm.html
4. www.uspto.gov/trademarkstrademarks/notices/international.jsp
5. http://tess2.uspto.gov/bin/gate.exe/f=login&p_lang=english&p_d=tmk
6. http://tess2.uspto.gov/tmdb/dscm/index.htm
7. www.thomasregister.com
8. www.dotcomdirectory.com/nsi/basic.htm
9. http://tess2.uspto.gov.tmdb/tmep/1000.htm and http://tess2.uspto.gov.tmdb/tmep/1900.htm
10. See United States Patent and Trademark Office, *Trademark Electronic Application System (TEAS)* (http://www.uspto.gov/teas/index.html) to file an application.

11. See United States Patent and Trademark Office, *Trademark Electronic Application System (TEAS)* (http://www.uspto.gov/teas/combinedpagesnew1.doc) to preview a filing before submission.

12. http://www.uspto.gov/trademarks/tm_fee_info.jsp

13. The product distributed by CreAgri contained, on average, 3 mg of the active ingredient hydroxytyrosol per dose though it was claimed that 25 mg was present. Title 21 of the Code of Federal regulations, Section 101 (21 CFR 101), requires that products claiming a certain content of substances such as the active ingredient named must contain AT LEAST that amount. CreAgri's Olivenol failed in this regard.

Chapter 3

1. See www.fi.edu/leraqn/.../edison-light-bulb.php/

2. www.unmuseum.org/lightbulbs.htm

3. *Ransom's Diamond Jewelry v. Steven Ransom* (24th Judicial Court, Parish of Jefferson, Louisiana, 2003); *Randazzo v. Randazzo et al.* (24th Judicial Court, Parish of Jefferson, Louisiana, 2009).

4. *Major League Properties, Inc. v. Sed Non Olet Denarius, Ltd.*, 817 F. Supp. 1103 (SDNY 1993).

5. *Dawn Donut Company, Inc. v. Hart's Food Stores, Inc.*, 267 F. 2d 358 (2d. Cir., 1959).

Chapter 4

1. Williamson, Harold F., *Winchester: the Gun That Won the West*, Combat Forces Press (1952, p. 169) (out of press).

2. http://www.uspto.gov/web/offices/ac/ido/oelp/taf/us_stat.htm

3. www.managingip.com/Article/2089405/Cost-and-duration-of-patent-litigation

Chapter 5

1. *Los Angeles News Service v. Tullo*, 9783 F. 2d. 791 (9th Cir., 1992).

2. Charles Dickens.

Chapter 6

1. 15 Rep. Pat. Cas., 105 (1898).

2. Schechter (1927).

3. *McDonald's Corporation v. Arche Technologies*, 17 U.S.P.Q. 2d 1557 (N. D. of Cal., 1990).

4. California Business and Professional Code Section 14330.

5. Lavin (1994), p. B1.

6. Keller (2000).

7. Supnik (1997), pp. 14–22.

8. Smith (2004).

9. *Eli Lilly & Co.*, 233 F3d. at 466; *Hormel Foods Corp.*, 73 F.3d at 506; also *Ringling Bros. Barnum and Bailey Combined Shows v. B.E. Windows Co.*, 937 F. Supp. 204, 209 (S.D. NY, 1006).

10. Tysver (2000); (www.bitlaw.com/trademark/dilution.html) p. 2.

11. *Deere and Co. v. MTD Products, Inc.*, 41 F.3d 39, 43 (2d Cir. 1994).

12. *Hasbro, Inc. v. Internet Entertainment Group, Inc.*, 40 U.S.P.Q. 2d. 1479 (W.D. Wash., 1996).

13. *Intermatic, Inc. v. Toeppen*, 947 F.Supp. 1227 (N.D. Ill., 1996).

14. *Anheuser-Busch, Inc. v. Andy's Sportswear*, 1996 U.S. Dist. Lexis 11583 (N. D. Cal. 1996).

15. *WAWA v. Haaf*, 40 U.S.P.Q. 2d. (BNA) 1629 (E. D. Pa. 1996).

16. *Mead Data Central, Inc. v. Toyota Motor Sales, Inc.* 702 F. Supp. 1309 (S. D. N. Y. 1988), reviewed 875 F. 2d. 1026 at 1028-29 (2d Circuit 1989).

17. *Icee Distributors, Inc. v. J & J Snack Foods Corp. and WalMart Stores, Inc.* (U.S. District Court, W. D. La., CV 99-0850S).

18. *Moseley d/b/a/ Victor's Little Secret v. Victoria's Secret Catalogue, Inc.*, Supreme Court Reporter 01-1015.

19. Gearan (2003).

20. *Nabisco, Inc. v. PF Brands, Inc.*, 51 U.S.P.Q. 2d 1882 (2000).

21. Banner (2000).

22. Ibid.

23. 68 U.S.L.W. 4217.

Chapter 7

1. http://www.uta.fi/~elna.m.eskola/pub.html

2. *Inwood Laboratories, Inc. v. Ives Laboratories, Inc.*, 456 US 844 (1982).

3. *Warner Brothers, Inc. v. Gay Toys, Inc.*, 724 F. 2d 327, 331 (2d. Cir. 1983).

4. Hoffman (n.d.) p. 1.

5. See *In Re Hudson News Company*, 39 USPQ 2d 1915 (TTAB 1996) and *In Re Bio-Medicus, Incorporated*, 31 USPQ 2d 1254 (TTAB 1994) for examples.

6. *Smith, Kline, and French Co. v. Premo Pharmaceutical Laboratories*, 481 F. Supp. 1184, 1187 (DNJ 1979).

7. *Two Pesos, Incorporated v. Taco Cabana, Incorporated* (505 US 763, 112 US 2753 (1992)).

8. *Fuddruckers, Incorporated v. Doc's B. R. Others, Incorporated*, 826 F. 2d 837, 846, 4 USPQ 2d 1026 (9 Cir. 1026) (1987).

9. *Pebble Beach Company v. Tour 18 I, Limited*, 942 F. Supp. 1513 (SD Tex.).

10. *Qualitex Co. v. Jacobson Products* (115 US 1300 (1995)).

11. *Par Pharmaceuticals, Inc. v. Searle Pharmaceuticals, Inc.* (227 USPQ 1024) (ND Ill. 1985) (Protection of blue tablet color).

12. *Merck Co. v. Par Pharmaceuticals, Inc.*, 770 F. 2d 1072 (3d Cir.).

13. *Abercrombie and Fitch Co. v. Hunting World, Inc.*, 537 F 2d. 4, 9 (2d Cir. 1976).

14. *Krueger International Inc. v. Nightingale Inc.*, 40 USPQ 2d, 1334, 1341 (SDNY 1996).

15. *Stuart Hall Co., Inc. v. Ampad Corp.* 51 F 3d, 780 (8th Cir 1995).

16. *Laureyssens v. Idea Group, Inc.*, 964 F. 2d. 131 (2d Cir. 1992).

17. *Knitwaves, Inc. v. Lollytogs Ltd.*, 71 F. 3d 996 (2d Cir. 1995).

18. *Sunbeam Products, Inc v. The West Bend Co.* 44 USPQ 2d (5th Cir. 1997).

19. *Artemide Sp.A. v. Grandlite Design and Manufacturing Co., Ltd.* 4 USPQ 2d 1915 (SDNY 1987).

20. *Ferrari Esercizio v. Roberts*, 944 F. 2d 1235 (6th Cir. 1991).

21. *Ferrari SpA v. McBurnie*, 11 USPQ 2d 1843 (SD Cal. (1989)).

22. *Callaway Golf Company v. Golf Clean, Inc.* 39 USPQ 2d 1737 (MD Fla. 1995).

23. *Sunbeam Products, Inc. v. West Bend Co*, 44 USPQ 2d 1161 (5th Cir. 1997).

24. *Toy Manufacturers v. Helmsley-Spear*, 960 F. Supp. 673 (SDNY 1997).

25. *Foxworthy v. Custom Tees, Inc.*, 879 F. Supp. 1200 (ND Ga. 1995)

26. *Carson v. Here's Johnny Portable Toilets, Inc.*, 498 F. Supp. 71 (ED Mich. 1980).

27. *Fotomat Corp. v. Houck* (166 USPQ 271 (Fla. Cir. Ct. 1970)).

28. 17 USPQ 2d. 1238 (TTAB 1990).

29. See *Vornado Air Circulation Systems, Inc. v. Duracraft Corp.*, 58 F. 3d 1498 (10th Cir. 1995) and prior actions; *Sears, Roebuck and Co. v. Stiffel Co.*, 376 US 225 (1964); *Compco Corp. v. Day-Brite Lighting, Inc.*, 376 US 234 (1964); and *Bonito Boats, Inc. v. Thunder Craft Boats, Inc.* 489 US 141 (1989).

Chapter 9

1. Harwit, Eric (1994), p. 208.

2. Ibid.

3. http://chinaautoweb.com/2011/01/chinese-auto-sales-set-new-world-record-of-18-million-units-in-2010/)

4. www.Chinacartimes.com
5. www.autoblog.com
6. www.beijing-08-preview
7. www.chinacartimes.com
8. www.chinacartimes.com
9. http://www.autonews.gasgoo.com
10. www.chinacarforums.com/

Chapter 10

1. http://www.constitution.ru/en/1000-3000-3.htm
2. Constitution of the Russian Federation, Sec. 1, Ch. 2, Arts. 17–64.
3. Zegelman, http://www.llrx.com/features/russiaiplaw.htm *Popular Press and Wire Sources.*
4. Curtis (1996).
5. Zegelman, Loc. Cit., pp. 5, 6.
6. United States Trade Representative, 2006 *Special 301 Report: Russian Federation.*
7. United States Trade Representative, 2006 *National Trade Estimate Report on Foreign Trade Barriers,* 554.
8. Katz and Ocheltree (2006).
9. *Saint Petersburg (Russia) Times* (2002, May 7).
10. www.europeancommission/euandtheworld/externaltrade/tradeissues/5october1006
11. Coalition for Intellectual Property Rights Press Release (2006, May 24).
12. Coalition for Intellectual Property Rights (2006).
13. AFX News Limited (2007, November 9).
14. Prime-Tass Business Newswire (2008, February 1).
15. RIA Novosti (2008, January 24).
16. www.columbiagazetteer.org/public/Russian%20federation.html
17. Ramirez (1990).
18. http://exchange.yahoo.com/currency (2012, May 9).
19. Kelly (2011).

References

AFX News Limited (2007, November 9). Russian police charge Brynsalov: A execs with illegal business activities.

Banner, B. E. (2000, April). Summaries of recent significant trademark and trade dress cases. www.banner.com

Blake, N. F. (2004). William Caxton (1414-24-1491). In *Oxford Dictionary of National Biography*. Oxford: Oxford University Press.

BYD Auto (2009, December 7). BYD SUV revealed! It's not a Lexus RV, it's not a Lexus RV. http://www.chinacartimes.com/2009/12/07/byd-suv-revealed-its-not-a-lexus-rv-its-not-a-lexus-rv/

BYD Auto (2009, April 14). BYD S8: Ready for the warm days. http://www.china cartimes.com/2009/04/14/byd-s8-convertible-ready-for-the-warm-days/

BYD Auto (2009, May 5). BYD T6: Is it Photoshop Tuesday at BYD? http://www.chinacartimes.com/2009/05/05/byd-t6-is-it-photoshop-tuesday/

Coalition for Intellectual Property Rights (2006). Part IV of the Russian Civil Code: Summary of key trademark protection issues.

Coalition for Intellectual Property Rights (2006, May 24). Six in ten owners say IP protection in Russia improved: Proposed part four of civil code widely feared. Press release.

Coca-Cola Company (2011, December 8). Coca-Cola moves its secret formula to the "world of Coca-Cola."

Curtis, G. E. (1996). *A country study: Russia*. Washingon, DC: General Printing Office for the Library of Congress.

Gao, G. (2009, May 26). Greek court rules against Daimler on China SUV. http://autonews.gasgoo.com/china-news/greek-court-rules-against-daimler-on-china-suv-090526.shtml

Gearan, A. (2003, March 4). Victoria's Secret loses case v. sex shop. *Kansas City Star Newspaper*.

Harwit, E. (1994). *China's automobile industry: Policies, problems, and prospects*. Armonk, NY: M. E. Sharpe, p. 208.

Hoffman, I. (n.d.). The protection of "trade dress." http://ivanhoffman.com/tradedress.html, p. 1.

Katz, S., & Ocheltree, M. (2006, October). *Intellectual property rights as a key obstacle to Russia's WTO accession*. Washington, DC: The Carnegie Endowment for International Peace.

Keller, K. L. (2000, January–February). The brand report card. *Harvard Business Review*, Reprint R100104.

Kelly, S. (2011). *Doing business in Russia—Industry overview.* Moscow: VM Consult.

Ladas, and Parry (n.d.). A brief history of the patent law of the United States. http://www.ladas.com/Patents/USPatentHistory/html, p. 32

Lavin, D. (February 16, 1994). A cloudy issue: Will ATM users be confused by a card called Cirrus? *Wall Street Journal,* p. B1.

McKinney Engineering Library, University of Texas (n.d.). U.S. trademark history timeline. www.lib.utexas.edu/engin/trademark/timeline/tmindex.html

Nunez, A. (2008, April 17). BYD e6 electrifies family hauling. http://www .autoblog.com/2008/04/17/beijing-08-preview-byd-e6-electrifies-family-hauling/

Paukert, C. (2009, January 13). BYD F3DM is the poor man's Toyota Corolla. http://www.autoblog.com/2009/01/13/detroit-2009-byd-f3dm-is-the-poor-mans-plug-in-toyota-corolla/

Pollard, A. W., & Redgrave G. R. (Eds.). (1976). *Short title catalog,* Second Volume. *The Bibliographical Society, 1976,* item 4920.

Prime-Tass Business Newswire (2008, February 1). Court orders company to remove Lukoil trademark from gas station.

Quinn, G. (2011, January 28). The cost of obtaining a patent in the United States. http://ipwatchdog.com/

Ramirez A. (1990, April 9). Pepsi will be bartered for ships and vodka in deal with Soviets. *New York Times.*

RIA Novosti (2008, January 24). Russia's envoy poised for military patent discussions with NATO.

Saint Petersburg (Russia) Times (2002, May 7). Fakes costing drug companies $250 million. www.europeancommission/euandtheworld/externaltrade/trade issues/5october1006

Schechter, F. I. (1927). The rational basis of trademark protection. *Harvard Law Review,* 40, 813.

Smith, L. T. (2004). Tarnishment and the FTDA: Lessening the capacity to identify and distinguish. *B. Y. U. Law Review,* 825, 828.

Supnik, P. D. (1997, May). Mark of distinction—A new federal law protects distinctive trademarks against dilution through unauthorized use. *Los Angeles Lawyer,* pp. 14–22.

Swarbrick, D. (2003). The Statute of Anne. www.swarb.co.uk/acts/1710Anne Statute.html

Tabber's Temptations (n.d.). History of trademark law. www.tabberone.com/trademarks/TrademarkLaw/ History/. p. 1.

The Intellectual Property Office of the United Kingdom (n.d.). The Licensing Act of 1662. www.ipo.gov.uk/types/copy/c-about/c-history

Tysver, D. A. (2000). Trademark dilution. Bitlaw: A Resource on Technology Law. www.bitlaw.com/trademark/dilution.html

United States Patent and Trademark Office. Acceptable identification of goods and services manual. http://tess.2.uspto.gov/netahtm/tidm.html

United States Patent and Trademark Office. International schedule of classes of goods and services. www.uspto.gov/trademarkstrademarks/notices/international.jsp

United States Patent and Trademark Office. T E S S (Trademark Electronic Search System). http://tess2.uspto.gov/bin/gate.exe/f=login&p_lang=english&p_d=tmk

United States Patent and Trademark Office. T E S S (Trademark Electronic Search System). *Design code manual.* http://tess2.udpto.gov/tmdb/dscm/index.htm

United States Patent and Trademark Office. *Trademark manual of examining procedure, chapter 1000 and 1900.* http://tess2.uspto.gov/tmdb/tmep/1000.htm and http://tess2.uspto.gov/ tmdb/tmep/1900.htm

Williamson, H. F. (1952). *Winchester: The gun that won the West.* Washington, DC: Combat Forces Press, p. 169.

Zegelman, J. (n.d.). Researching intellectual property law in the Russian Federation. *Popular Press and Wire Sources* (LLRX, Inc.). Accessible at http://www.llrx.com/features/russiaiplaw.htm

Index

OTHER TITLES IN OUR STRATEGIC MANAGEMENT COLLECTION

William Q. Judge, Old Dominion University,
Collection Editor

- *Building Strategy and Performance Through Time: The Critical Path* by Kim Warren
- *A Leader's Guide to Knowledge Management: Drawing on the Past to Enhance Future Performance* by John Girard
- *An Executive's Primer on the Strategy of Social Networks* by Mason Carpenter
- *Succeeding at the Top: A Self-Paced Workbook for Newly Appointed CEOs and Executives* by Bernard Liebowitz
- *Fundamentals of Global Strategy: A Business Model Approach* by Cornelis de Kluyver
- *Operational Leadership* by Andrew Spanyi
- *Dynamic Strategies for Small Businesses* by Sviatoslav Steve Seteroff
- *Strategic Analysis and Choice: A Structured Approach* by Alfred Warner
- *Business Intelligence: Making Decisions Through Data Analytics* by Jerzy Surma
- *Designing the Networked Organization* by Ken Everett
- *Moral Leadership: A Transformative Model for Tomorrow's Leaders* by Cam Caldwell

Announcing the Business Expert Press Digital Library

Concise E-books Business Students Need for Classroom and Research

This book can also be purchased in an e-book collection from your library as

- a one-time purchase,
- that is owned forever,
- allows for simultaneous readers,
- has no restrictions on printing, and
- can be downloaded as PDFs from within the library community.

Our digital library collections are a great solution to beat the rising cost of textbooks. e-books can be loaded into their course management systems or onto student's e-book readers.

The **Business Expert Press** digital libraries are very affordable, with no obligation to buy in future years. For more information, please visit **www.businessexpertpress.com/librarians**. To set up a trial in the United States, please contact **Adam Chesler** at *adam.chesler@businessexpertpress .com* for all other regions, contact **Nicole Lee** at *nicole.lee@igroupnet.com*.

www.ingramcontent.com/pod-product-compliance
Lightning Source LLC
Chambersburg PA
CBHW050121210326
41519CB00015BA/4049